Chinese Customs and Wisdoms

Inesa Pleskacheuskaya

FOREIGN LANGUAGES PRESS

First Edition 2007

Home Page:
http://www.flp.com.cn

E-mail Addresses:
Info@flp.com.cn
Sales@flp.com.cn

ISBN 978- 7-119-04242-8
©Foreign Languages Press, Beijing, 2007
Published by
Foreign Languages Press
24 Baiwanzhuang Road, Beijing 100037, China
Distributed by
China International Book Trading Corporation
35 Chegongzhuang Xilu, Beijing 100044, China
P.O.Box 399, Beijing, China

Printed in the People's Republic of China

Contents

Traditional China 3

The Main Value • *101*

Everlasting Feast • *137*

Traditional China

An Ancient Country in the East

China is a wonderful country. The whole world and history revolve around it — at least it is what the locals think. In many aspects they are right as years, centuries and even millennia didn't seriously alter outer boundaries of the country. For almost four thousand years China has occupied nearly the same territory. Centuries and wars didn't change the main thing the Chinese thought about itself: This is the vast Celestial Country, the state situated right in the centre of the world. It is

Forbidden City: residence of the Chinese emperors for 500 years.

Millions of people from all over the world come to Xi'an, ancient capital of China, to see the "eighth wonder of the world" — Terra-cotta Warriors defending the mausoleum of the first emperor of China Qin Shi Huang.

exactly how the name of the country is translated — the Middle Kingdom.

The state became united for the first time during the rule of Emperor Qin Shi Huang (259-210 BC). Literally, Qin Shi Huang means "the first emperor of the Qin Dynasty." He spent nine years conquering (he preferred to think — uniting) six independent kingdoms. He personally appointed and dismissed his representatives in the provinces. Qin Shi Huang's tomb with the terra-cotta army is still impressive and justly regarded as one of the world's wonders. There are around 7,500 full-length warriors, all with unique facial expressions. So, you can imagine the ambitious nature of the ruler. No wonder he initiated the construction of the biggest engineering project in the ancient history, the Great Wall. The Wall was declared mainly for the purpose of guarding against nomadic tribes from north. Actually the Great Wall didn't provide necessary protection but it strengthened territorial unanimity of the country and promoted the unique Chinese civilization.

Experts are unanimous that this civilization got its main distinctive features during the Han Dynasty (206 BC-AD 220) when the state adopted the Confucius' doctrine as its official ideology. Great attention was paid to education and the first university was

established in the 2nd century BC. Education is very important in modern China and Confucius is still regarded as the greatest teacher. Other important steps made during the Han Dynasty were: taxes decreased as incentive for economic development, free trade encouraged, single currency and standardized weights and measures system introduced for the first time in history. People of the country called themselves Hans and it is the name of the biggest ethnic group of the modern China.

Ancient China saw flourishing

The Great Wall of China today is one of the main attractions.

science and technology. The Chinese acquired ac-knowledge of iron smelting 1,500 years before Europeans; they invented gun-powder that was introduced to Europe 300 years later; book-printing was spreading all over China since the 11th century. By the 13th century a simple loom was invented; mathematicians deduced algebra and trigonometry theorems unknown to Europeans during the next 300 years. Moreover, don't forget the compass invented in China in the 4th century BC. Do you know when Europe managed to know it? 1,500 years later! People in China widely used paper in the 2nd century BC already and it was in China that the paper money was first introduced. Paper appeared in Europe 14 centuries later. The Chinese built first oil derricks in the 1st century BC — 1,900 years earlier than in Europe. The ancient country used oil and gas as fuel in the 4th century BC, again, 14 centuries earlier than in Europe. I didn't even mention yet such usual domestic devices as a spinning-rod (2nd century BC in China, 14 centuries later in Europe), an umbrella (4th century BC and 1,200 years later in Europe) and matches (577 and millennia later in Europe). As economists estimated, the medieval China was the richest state of the time; per capita GDP in the Europe was just a quarter from that of China's.

At the end of the 17th century China was a stable

Painted clay figurine, Han Dynasty.

Compass, Han Dynasty.

society with a sufficient economy and a population of more than 300 million people — more than that of the whole Europe. Many modern Western historians agree that during the reign of Emperor Qianlong (r. 1736-1796) China was the richest and the most prosperous country of the world.

The Chinese executive system was as before strongly influenced by the Confucius' ideas such as that power and high official status must belong not to the rich and noble but to cultural and intellectual elite. Word *shenshi* meant both official and intelligent person. Humanitarian knowledge was valued much more than technical abilities; for getting an assignment it was necessary to pass difficult exams and demonstrate knowledge of classical, historical and philosophical works, poetry and calligraphy. The names of those emerged top in the imperial examinations can be seen today in the Beijing's Temple of Confucius, some of the inscriptions are of 1,300-1,400 years old. After retirement officials usually returned to their hometowns teaching children and working in the interests of the community. For the China's 300 million people there were 27,000 officials.

Earthquake Sensor invented by Zhang Heng, Han Dynasty.

It seems that as early as in the 14th century China was at the verge of the industrial revolution like the one that took

Confucius giving a lecture.

place in England 400 years later. But the development was suspended and historians are still discussing the reasons. There are actually several of them. Population increased rapidly and great number of cheap labor force didn't promote inventions of new machines and other technical improvements. Another factor of no small importance is that the nearly perfect bureaucratic system absorbed the best human resources thus depriving other fields including science off lucid minds. And finally, there came the Mongol invasion. However, that period of time was not exclusively negative for the development of China. Under the Mongolian emperors (they ruled in China as the Yuan Dynasty, 1279-1368), construction of the Grand Canal connecting the North and the South was

Confucius.

Peking Opera performance staged by students and teachers of the National Academy of Chinese Theatre Arts.

completed, foreign trade was active. Famous Venetian merchant and traveler Marco Polo lived in China during the reign of Khublai Khan and described the country as highly developed and a rich state.

Before the premiere.

Meanwhile Europe approached. Goods from the Kingdom of Heaven, i.e., China, such as silk, porcelain and tea were in high demand in the West. Europeans were greatly attracted by China's huge market. But it was not that easy to get into the desired market for the Western countries as China had stringent restrictions for contacts with the outside world. Foreign trade was carried out through just one port, Canton (Guanzhou), and the foreign merchants suffered a lot from despotism of the local officials.

First attempts of the British delegations to establish diplomatic relations with China and to carry out commercial activities failed. The emperor gave a cordial welcome to the Ambassador George McCartney but refused his proposals by saying that China possessed everything it actually needed and that the country was not interested in imported goods. Thus it is natural that Chinese export prevailed over import. The British Parliament in 1784 approved tax decrease on tea import thus making it the Albion's national drink. It virtually drained the country's supply of silver as it was the main currency for payments in the China-UK trade.

The experienced British merchants didn't waste their time looking for a product that could be in a great demand in China. That was opium. For many centuries it had been used in China as medicine but since the 18th century its narcotic characteristics has been made widely known. Ruinous habit spread quickly starting from the upper class — officials and the elite.

Narco cartels? Columbian barons, the "golden triangle" and Afghan opium? All this appeared

Old Town of Pingyao included into the UNESCO World Heritage. It is the only city of China with intact Ming-dynasty city wall. Time seems to stand still here — you can experience old China in all its brilliance.

later but the world's first narcotic business was created by the famous Ost-Indian Company which monopolized poppy production in India. More than 10 percent of the company's profit was made from opium trade. Because of the narcotic the trade balance changed quickly, this time in favor of Britain — despite China's increasing export. Profits of Britons taken from the opium trade surpassed its total import of silk and tea. In 1820-1840 China exported goods worth in total 10 million *liang* (= 50 grams) of silver and imported goods worth of 60 million *liang*, most of them were drugs.

By 1840s the number of drug addicts in China reached an incredible figure of two million and the authorities sounded the alarm. In 1839 Lin Zexu, the representative of the central government in Guanzhou, declared state of war to opium traders by emptying their warehouses and destroying goods worth in total of 10 million *liangs* of silver. The Britain's reply was fast and violent — military squadron. This is how the First Opium War started. The Chinese troops were defeated and in 1842 the Treaty of Nanjing was signed. China actually partly lost its sovereignty as a huge indemnity was imposed on Beijing, four ports were opened for foreign trade and Hong Kong Island was handed over to Britain to stay under the British administration for more than 150 years. The foreign juris-

diction was established over the Chinese customs system.

The results of the Second Opium War (1856-1860) were even worse for China. Besides Britain, France, the USA, Russia and later Germany and Japan struggled for their shares thus dividing China into zones of interests.

Soon after those dramatic events, part of the Chinese elite called for in-depth study of the Western experience and mastering it on the local soil, they demanded wide reforms and the country's modernization.

Under the influence of these movements in 1860-1890 the authorities implemented "self-enhancement practice" targeted on fortifying the defensive potential; they built arsenals for pro-

Carvings in relief of the Monument of the People's Heroes on Tiananmen Square, describing the ban of opium.

duction of weapons under foreign licenses, shipbuilding yards for building modern ships, started army reorganization, built coal mines and railways.

Private business was on the rise. In 1870s-1890s, more than 70 private enterprises were established employing around 30,000 people. But foreign states thought themselves the real masters of the country and they didn't welcome such changes. In 1892 they barred the Chinese businessmen from establishing private enterprises for the next 10 years. The customs was as before under the foreigners' administration; import taxes were more than twice lower than export taxes. At the end of the 19th century, of 600 foreign companies operating in China, more than 100 were industrial enterprises.

The year of 1911 witnessed the unavoidable collapse of the Qing Empire. It was crushed by internal contradictions, population growth, technological backwardness, foreign interventions and corruption. The civil war and then Japanese occupation followed.

Victory of the Communists under Mao Zedong in 1949 brought new tests for China, namely industrialization and collectivization, "Big Leap Forward" and "The Great Proletarian Cultural Revolution." Thus real stabilization in the country commenced only in the beginning of the 1980s after Deng Xiaoping with his famous saying "it

Bronze galloping horse, Eastern Han Dynasty.

Tiananmen Square and rostrum in Beijing. Standing on this very rostrum on October 1, 1949 Mao Zedong declared establishment of the new country — the People's Republic of China.

doesn't matter what color a cat is if it is able to catch a mice" which was firmly established on the China's political arena. Political reforms and opening-up policy keep going on nowadays. China today is one of the most dynamically developing countries of the world, playing an important role in international political, economic and cultural relations. Walking on streets of Chinese cities, you will clearly see — the country is on rise, it has already overcome the most difficult times. The Chinese history teaches: There is always a rise after a fall. Fortunately, this law is as inevitable as the sunrise.

Five Elements of the Chinese Universe

The Chinese notion best known to the West is that of *yin* and *yang*, opposite but coexisting principles forming the whole Universe. The words themselves originally meant respectively shady and sunny mountain slopes but in philosophical sense they include wide range of opposing pairs — dark and light, wet and dry, female and male, weak and strong, dead and alive etc. By the way, bad and good doesn't necessarily include in such pairing and doesn't directly oppose to each other.

At about the same time that the notion of *yin* and *yang* started to include not only two mountain slopes but was being extended to include all beings, another principle that would have even greater implications for the Chinese worldview appeared.

Symbol of Taoism: Diagram of cosmological scheme.

For a long time the Chinese believed that the world was divided into four parts: Azure Dragon, White Tiger, Red Bird and Black Turtle; east, west, south, north; spring, autumn, summer and winter. By the early 3rd century BC this idea had been transformed into a conception of five elements — and since those distant days this idea governed people's minds in the Kingdom of Heaven. This transformation was very likely originally achieved by the addition of the "center" as the fifth basic element. This is how conception of *wu xing* — five elements, namely wood, fire, earth, metal and water, composing the Universe — came into being.

Taoists thought that the world was divided into *yin* and *yang* that gave birth to five elements. From those five elements ten thousand things — *wan wu* — appear. "Ten thousand" for the ancient Chinese was the infinite aggregate, i.e., everything existing under Heaven.

Five elements are not to be understood as real substances but rather as sorts of constantly evolving energy, in some sense symbols for certain basic characteristics of matter. Nature of water is to moisten and to flow downward; of fire — to heat and to rise; of wood — to

Stone statue of Lao Zi, creator of Taoist doctrines, on Qingyuan Mountain, Fujian Province.

bend and straighten again; of metal — to be cast or hammered into various forms; of earth — to fertile. At the time of the Warring States Period (475-221 BC), the notion arose that the elements not only gave rise to each other but also might destroy each other. Wood could give rise to fire, fire to earth, earth to metal, metal to water and water to wood. In accordance with another conception, water could conquer fire, fire vanquish metal, metal destroy wood, wood

The *Yin-yang* symbol is a popular motif, often used to decorate Chinese houses. The picture shows such a symbol on the wall of the Chang family mansion, Shanxi Province.

conquer earth and earth overcome water.

With time every aspect of life was interpreted within the five elements theory. All five elements became related to the seasons of the year, colors, cardinal points, flavors, numbers, internal organs, etc.

The succession of the seasons of the year is reflected by the interdependence of the five elements: in spring, wood is dominant and gives rise to fire which is the element of summer. Fire gives rise to earth, which is characteristic of the center — the third month of summer. Earth, in turn, gives rise to metal which dominates autumn, and metal — to the water of winter.

Each element has its corresponding color, flavor and cardinal point. The north, black color and salty flavor correspond to water; the south, red and bitter taste to fire; the east, green and sour taste to wood. Metal corresponds to the west, white color and hot flavor; earth is the centre, yellow color and sweet taste.

As applied to humans the five elements are connected with various organs of the body and certain emotions which are of great importance for the traditional Chinese medicine. Wood is related to the eyes, the sinews, the gall bladder, the liver and anger; fire to the tongue, the blood vessels, the small intestine, the heart and the feeling of joy; earth to the mouth, the muscles, the stomach, the pancreas and worrying; metal to the nose, the hairs of the body, the large intestine, the lungs and sadness; and water to the ears, the bones, the bladder, the kidneys and fear.

The *Yin-Yang* School allocated numbers to each of the five elements: 1 and 6 to water, 2 and 7 to fire, 3 and 8 to wood, 4 and 9 to metal, 5 and 10 to earth. Even numbers are regarded to be Earth numbers and odd numbers are Heaven's. Odd numbers give rise to the element and the even numbers bring it to perfection and fruition. These relationships are reflected in the famous *Book of Changes* (*I Ching*).

The five elements theory was also applied to history. The most famous representative of the *Yin-Yang* School was philosopher Zhou Yen who lived in the 3rd century BC. He thought that the succession of the various dynasties imitated that of the elements. Earth, under which sign the legendary ancestor of the Chinese nation Huangdi (the Yellow Emperor) ruled, was conquered by wood, sign of the Xia Dynasty (2070-1600 BC). This in turn was vanquished by the Shang Dynasty (1600-1046 BC) whose sign was metal. Zhou Yen thought that fire of the Zhou Dynasty (1046-256 BC), during which he lived, would be conquered by water of a next dynasty thus starting a new historical cycle. Every dynasty adopted the color of patronizing sign, changed ideals and even adapted the calendar — everything in accordance with one of the five basic elements.

In Taoist philosophy, the term *zhen wu* means not only the five elements but also their ability to drive away evil spirits. That is why the five elements were often used in *fengshui* as protection. Even in present-day Beijing, it is possible to see how emperors of the Ming (1368-1644) and Qing (1644-1911) dynasties used *zhen wu* for defending their capital from evil spirits and enemies.

In the east of Beijing — which is corresponding direction of the element of wood — *zhen wu* was represented by the Royal Timber Mill outside the city wall of Guangqumen. It was here that timber was prepared for building the royal palaces. It was widely believed that the timber was imbued with supernatural powers hence the place got the name the Sacred Timber Mill. The section of *nanmu* wood measured more than 23 meters in length and more than 2 meters in diameter was kept here. In 1758, Emperor Qianlong wrote the "Song of the Sacred Timber" detailing

The statue of the smiling Maitreya with a paunch can be found in many places in China.

the history of the wood. He also ordered a pavilion to be built to house a stone tablet on which the words of the "Song" were carved.

In the south which equates to fire, outside the city wall near Yongdingmen, the Yan Dun, or Smoke Mound, stood. It was a beacon tower, in which fire was lit as an alarm during wars. The tower was built first at the times when modern Beijing was known as Dadu (1271-1368) and was rebuilt in the Ming Dynasty in the shape of a pyramid. During the Qing Dynasty the tower was reconstructed once again, a pavilion was added housing a stone pillar with two articles by Emperor Qianlong. In those articles he described customs of the vicinity and the construction survey of the capital, and now this pillar is recognized as an important historical monument. Up to 1900 the Qing emperors held ceremonies here to offer sacrifices to the gods of fire and water.

The element of metal corresponds to the west, thus local *zhen wu* is the Big Bell of the Jueshen Temple, often referred to as the

King of Ancient Bells.

The bell was cast during the rule of Emperor Zhu Di (reign name is Yongle, 1403-1424) from the Ming Dynasty. It was seen as a symbol of courage and intelligence of the emperor who transferred the capital from the southern Nanjing to the northern Beijing as well as a mark of respect to his soldiers. The bell measures 6.95 meters in height, 4 meters in diameter and weights 26.5 tons. Both the interior and exterior are inscribed with around 100 Buddhist sutras containing more than 230,000 Chinese characters.

The Big Bell was originally kept in Beihai Park, then it was moved to the Wanshou Temple and finally during the Qing Dynasty to the Juesheng Temple, which now is the Museum of Ancient Bells.

Many believe that the *zhen wu* of the north which corresponds to the element of water is Kunming Lake in the Sum-

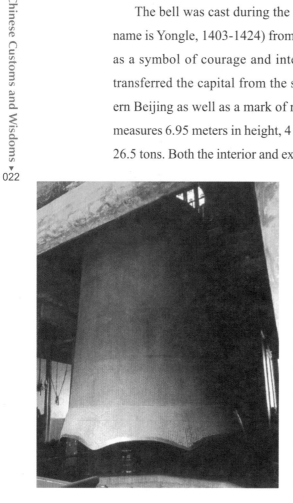

Yongle Bell in the Big Bell Temple Museum.

mer Palace. Long ago the lake had a name of Weng after the name of the man-made hill. Emperor Qianlong renamed it as Wanshou Hill, as one of his birthday presents to his mother. The lake was named Kunming after a story about a Han Dynasty (206 BC-220 AD) emperor named Liu Che, who dug a lake to train his

navy. Thanks to the training the imperial forces conquered Kunming State in today's Yunnan Province. By renaming it Kunming Lake, Qianlong expressed confidence that his reign would be as strong as that of the Han Dynasty emperors.

Kunming Lake in the Summer Palace is *zheng wu* of the capital's north. It symbolically defended Beijing from evil spirits and other inauspicious developments.

Earth equates to the centre, and the corresponding *zhen wu* is Jingshan, the hill behind the Forbidden City. During the Yuan Dynasty (1279-1368) it was a small hill with Yanchun Tower on its top. When the Forbidden City was constructed the earth excavated to create the canals and lakes around it was used to form Wansui (Longevity) Hill which was in full accordance with the local *fengshui*. Heaping the earth over the old tower of the Yuan Dynasty was seen by the Ming rulers as symbolically burying the previous

The Stone Boat on the Kunming Lake.

dynasty. However, in 1644 this hill with deep symbolical meaning became the death place for the last Ming emperor — Chongzheng hang himself on a tree at the foot of the hill. The circle locked.

Eleven years later, the Qing emperor renamed the hill Jingshan and Emperor Qianlong built five pavilions on the hill — in fair weather from here, the Forbidden City lies before the eyes in all its grandeur.

Chinese Festivals: Keeping Traditions Alive

We all love holidays and the happy gatherings of family and friends that they bring, and the Chinese are no exception. The Chinese celebrate festivals based on the lunar calendar dating back thousands of years. The most popular favourite is Lunar New Year, or Spring Festival, which falls on the first day of the first lunar month.

Spring Festival, or *chunjie*, dates back to the Western Zhou Dynasty (1121-771 BC). Two weeks beforehand, a feeling of pleasurable holiday antici-pation permeates the atmosphere. Everything must be prepared just so: music on the streets, deco-rations and illuminations.

New Year decorations are very popular.

What I most like about China is that its ancient traditions are still very much alive. Many people, espe-cially those living in countryside, still celebrate *chunjie* in the traditional manner. This means buying something new to wear, even if it is only a new handker-chief or scarf. In the old days, the holiday was a huge celebration because for

Chinese houses are decorated with auspicious designs like this for the lunar New Year.

many it was the only day of the year they allowed themselves the luxury of eating meat. It is no longer a delicacy, and many Chinese can afford to present to their family members and friends extravagantly impractical gifts like flowers. In Beijing alone in 2005 more than 100 million fresh cut flowers were sold during the seven-day holiday.

On the Spring Festival Eve, all family members get together, even when separated by thousands of kilometers. Transportation companies consequently rake in high profits in the days leading up to it, as almost all of China is on the move.

As it was originally the main meal of the year, *chunjie* dinner has many different dishes to choose from, but you will see the crescent moon-shaped dumplings (*jiaozi*) in every household in northern China. Dumplings that have

Before the lunar New Year all doors should be decorated with *chunlian* — poems with good wishes and with character *fu* (happiness) turned upside down.

Picture of Door God posted on the front door of a house to ward off evil spirits on the occasion of lunar New Year. It is still practised in the countiyside.

been prepared in advance and traditionally the only dish served in the first five days of the New Year, as in Chinese the words "stir-fry" and "to quarrel" are both pronounced "*chao.*" This is why women avoid cooking during the first week of the Lunar New Year as they don't want to use that word to their loved ones. These traditional precautions are a boon to China's catering industry as that week restaurants are solidly booked several months in advance.

Another "must" dish on the festive table is fish, again, because of pronunciation. In Chinese the words "fish" and "surplus" sound similar, so those

who have had fish on the festivals might find wealth in the coming year. As one who would not even try to resist the temptation of such easily gained riches, I also have fish on my festive table — just in case.

On the night of *chunjie* people celebrate by rushing outside and setting off firecrackers. As it is impossible to sleep that night, the best thing to do is join in, as I usually do. In downtown areas of big cities like Beijing, firecrackers are restricted, but as people find it impossible to celebrate Spring Festival without them, many drive out of the capital to the outskirts and have fun making lots of noise.

During the first week of the Spring Festival celebrations, villages, towns and cities heave with festivities and performances. Traditional Lion, Dragon, Boat and Mermaid dances are very popular, as are acrobatics, traditional opera performances, and street-traders selling everything from pictures to sweets to sundry souvenirs. Years ago these activities took place

Fish is a "must" dish during the lunar New Year festivities, because of pronunciation. In Chinese the words "fish" and "surplus" sound similar, so those from a household serving fish might find wealth in the coming year.

around temples, and are still known as temple fairs.

On April 5, 105 days after the winter solstice there is another important festival, *qingming*. This day reminds me of the traditional Slavonic Radunitsa festival, when people go to cemeteries to pay their respects to beloved family members who have passed

away. In China people do the same and more — they leave special sacrificial paper money on tombs, or tie it to nearby trees. Those far away from their ancestors' tombs and unable to return burn sacrificial money and other paper objects wherever they are.

According to the Chinese lunar calendar, autumn occurs in the seventh, eighth and ninth lunar months. That's why Mid-Autumn Festival, *zhongqiu*, another important occasion when all the family gathers, is celebrated on the 15th day of the 8th lunar month when the moon is at its brightest.

This holiday, when families gather in courtyards and share a special meal of round eatables like oranges, pomegranates (whose seeds symbolize many children), melons and — last but not least — moon cakes (*yuebing*), has been celebrated in China since the Tang Dynasty (618-907).

The first stalls selling *yuebing* appeared more than a thousand years ago in the then capital city of Chang'an (modern Xi'an). Today *yuebing* are the traditional Chinese dessert, they have become the profitable industry. Insiders

On the *Qingming* Festival, people go to the tombs of their deceased dear ones to pay their respect.

During the traditional Mid-Autumn Festival people present each other moon cakes (*yuebings*).

say that during holiday week *yuebing* makers earn around 80 percent of their yearly income. For example, Shanghai consumes 10,000 tons of moon cakes in just one week!

For me all these Chinese festivals represent an organic connection between venerated themes and traditions and China's current rapid development. In carrying on the customs of their ancestors from centuries ago and celebrating ancient festivals, fast-moving China brings new life into them.

Emotions of Rabbits and Courage of Pigs

Having arranged to meet a friend of mine from the Netherlands for lunch in downtown Beijing recently, we both turned up wearing exactly the same color and style of sweaters. After remarking on this coincidence we forgot it, but at our next lunch we found that our pocket books were of the same color — red. On closer investigation of each other's backgrounds, it became apparent that many of our idiosyncrasies, reactions to situations and life experiences are the same, despite that we had been brought up in totally different environments. It eventually transpired that we were both born in the Chinese year of Rooster. Whether you believe in the Chinese zodiac or not, in our case it explained everything.

So, what is the Chinese zodiac? And why is it in vogue to the extent that people in Europe and the U.S. want to know everything about it?

Ancient Chinese took animal zodiac signs very seriously, sometimes using them to decide matters of life and death. Detailed horoscopes have always been a vital aspect of arranged marriages. Tragic partings and broken hearts often followed the discovery that a couple intending to marry had signs in direct opposition, for example, Pig and Dog, Monkey and Rooster, or Tiger and Rabbit.

For centuries Chinese people have believed that **Rats** bring

wealth and take every possible opportunity to prosper. People of this sign (born in 1948, 1960, 1972, 1984, 1996, etc.) are family-oriented, always the life and soul of every party and company, and generous for loved ones. They are good traders, writers and publicists.

The unpretentious, uncompromising **Ox** (1949, 1961, 1973, 1985, 1997, etc.) works hard no matter what obstacles or difficulties it is confronted by. Sometimes described as obstinate, the Ox is simply persistent. Its attributes are devotion and diligence. Many outstanding surgeons, servicemen and barbers were born under Ox auspices.

Chinese consider the **Tiger** (1950, 1962, 1974, 1986, 1998, etc.) rather than a lion as king of all animals, so it is no surprise that people of this sign become respected and feared leaders. They are powerful and courageous, but also sensitive, emotional and passionate. Many well-known business tycoons, researchers and athletes are Tigers.

The helplessly emotional **Rabbit** (1951, 1963, 1975, 1987, 1999, etc.) symbolizes faithfulness. People of this sign are intelligent, well mannered and hate discord. They are sensitive, cautious creatures, many of whom are successful businessmen, lawyers, diplomats and actors.

The **Dragon** (1952, 1964, 1976, 1988, 2000, etc.) is the most auspicious of all creatures of the zodiac. It has

special significance for symbolizing the Chinese nation. It is therefore no wonder that one of the most outstanding figures in China's contemporary history — Deng Xiaoping — was born in the year of Dragon. Many readers have undoubtedly seen Bruce Lee's cult movie *Enter the Dragon* but may be surprised to know that this actor/martial arts expert was also a Dragon.

A person born a Dragon is proud, self-confident, smart and often egoistic. They are intelligent and strive for perfection in everything — from aesthetically pleasing home to their partners in love, but most of all in the work. Many famous artists, clergymen and - as already mentioned — politicians, are Dragons.

According to legend, the mythical half-human and half-snake brother and sister Fu Xi and Nü Wa were genitors of the Chinese race. This is why the **Snake** (1953, 1965, 1977, 1989, 2001, etc.) is also a very strong sign (Mao Zedong was a Snake). People born in this year are believed to be wise, intuitive, usually softly speaking deep thinkers. As snakes change their skin, so people born this year frequently change their jobs and spheres of interest. Fascinated with the unknown and eager to try everything, they succeed in the least expected fields. Snakes are great teachers, philosophers, writers and psychiatrists.

The Chinese probably most admire people born in the year of **Horse** (1954, 1966, 1978, 1990, 2002, etc.) for their energy and open-mindedness. They easily make friends and maintain long and harmonious relationships. People born these years like to travel, see new places and generally be where action is. Their ability to work long and hard is impressive. People born under this sign often become scientists, poets and politicians.

Chinese people associate **Sheep** (1955, 1967, 1979, 1991, 2003, etc.) with peace, and those born under this sign are expected to be friendly and good team workers. Westerners consider sheep as silly but Chinese see them as having strong beliefs and deep compassion. People born in this year are creative, easy going, and have a lively imagination and dry humor. They make fine actors, gardeners and archeologists.

Monkey (1956, 1968, 1980, 1992, 2004, etc.) is one of the most beloved species in China. The Monkey is believed to be smart and a great intriguer. Those born under this sign are curious, observant and have the ability to solve the most complex problems. Monkey people generally succeed in any sphere of activity they choose.

Rooster (1957, 1969, 1981, 1993, 2005, etc.) is active, ambitious and talented. It is hopeless a dreamer but always ready to fight for his or her beliefs. People of this sign are decisive and hard

working, but they achieve the best results when working alone. Roosters enjoy working as restaurateurs, journalists, travelers and servicemen.

Dog (1958, 1970, 1982, 1994, 2006, etc.) is a loyal and easygoing friend and associated with justice. People born this year are intolerant of injustice and always ready to help those less fortunate. They may be successful businessmen, political activists, teachers and — watch out! — spies.

The modest and fortunate **Pig** (1959, 1971, 1983, 1995, 2007, etc.) likes fun but is not afraid of hard work. In China Pig typifies courage. People born under this sign are diligent, always well informed and reliable, but sometimes naive as they expect the same from others. Pigs are born peacemakers; they make good showmen and lawyers.

It is up to you whether or not to believe in your sign. As for me I treat the Chinese zodiac with respect and so benefit from it. For example, it says that two Roosters under one roof make life unbearable for each other. My mom is also a Rooster, but believe me, she is my best friend. Could this be because I take note of what my zodiac says and live under a different roof from her?

Want to Be Happy? Consult Wind and Water

People all over the world love their homes and desire a happy family life. Chinese people are no different, but have the enviable capacity to place and arrange their homes in a manner that guarantees auspiciousness for the whole family. This know-how is based on the art or science of *fengshui*, literally wind and water.

Fengshui became a generally known term in the West about 20 years ago. Today it is a source of fascination to thousands, as may be seen from the shelves full of books on it in the "new age" section of any bookshop, and heavy patronage of courses on this ancient discipline.

There is now overwhelming and widespread belief in the efficacy of *fengshui*. World famous developer Donald Trump consulted a Chinese *fengshui* master on one of his projects — the Western

Just behind the entrance to many old Chinese houses you can find a decorative screen. People believe that evil spirits move only directly, so, according to *fengshui* theory if you erect a screen on their way, they will be unable to enter the house.

Gulf Building in New York's south Central Park. On following the advice and guidelines proffered, he immediately sold this former white elephant, and at a handsome profit too. This is just one example of what many people now acknowledge — that there are phenomena in life and nature that cannot be analyzed or explained by Western science. Within the realm of ancient Chinese wisdom, all that is needed to benefit from *fengshui* is an open mind.

Old Town of Pingyao (Shanxi Province) was built strictly in accordance with all *fengshui* demands. The tallest building in the town is Shilou tower, and it marks the centre of the town.

Fengshui combines astronomy, topography and environmental science with architecture, botany, ethics and divination. It has been an integral part of Chinese culture for almost 4,000 years. There is still debate as to whether it is a science or an art, and whether it requires specialized knowledge or just intuitiveness. In my view, it constitutes a set of guidelines on living. Sometimes they are just common sense, like wearing a safety helmet on a construction site. But the deeper one looks into *fengshui*, the more apparent its complexity.

The word *fengshui* consists of two parts. "*Fen*" means wind, as well as breath of life or style. "*Shui*" is water; it is one of the main elements of the universe, the essential principle of life. River in the Taoist philosophy is embodiment of Tao stream which is

Lijiang City (Yunnan Province) is another example of *fengshui* usage. The main characteristics of the city are mountains and water.

Batik is traditional Chinese craft, very popular nowadays all over the world.

the innermost essence of the objective reality. Chinese poet compared *fengshui* to water ripples in which the sage was able to see and read signs not evident to the uninitiated. *Fengshui* master is able to feel presence of *qi* energy, invisible forces of nature in living and still objects, in rocks, water reservoirs and plants.

Fengshui originated in the Zhou Dynasty (1027-777 BC). Its purpose was to find auspicious sites for graves before being used to find appropriate dwelling sites for the living. This is how *fengshui* came to figure so largely in the building of houses and settlements.

As a code of principles and rules *fengshui*

was formed in the 12th-13th centuries during the Song Dynasty when Wang Zi and other scientists formulated the conception. At the same time Fujian (school of compass) and Jiangxi (school of form) schools appeared. The main tool for the Fujian school was a special geomantic compass. The Jiangxi school interpreted living forces of the earth, analyzing landscape with special emphasis put on mountains and water sources as they were considered to be the dragon's blood arteries. This school is still very influential in the southern China.

The main *fengshui* principle is Taoist belief in a single whole: heaven, earth and mankind are in interrelation. The key to harmonious and happy life is coexistence of a man and nature in an ideal environment.

When applied to architecture, Chinese geomancy can appear somewhat reactionary. In the past, farmers cited *fengshui* when protesting construction projects in their territory. Chinese were suspicious of European-built railways and regarded the shadows of Christian churches as detrimental to the environment. Belief in the discipline was so strong that the direction of railroads was accordingly changed and the height of church spires adjusted so as to stay in harmony with the local *fengshui*.

Naxi people created unique Dongba culture and the writing system which have no analogues in the world. (Lijiang Town)

Masters of *fengshui* were, and still are, consulted when choosing the appropriate date for wedding or funeral, and commissioned

Classical gardens of Suzhou included into the UNESCO World Heritage are famous all over the world for their amazing landscape design and usage of *fengshui* elements.

to write prayers that act as amulets.

Air, light, the angle at which the sun rises, level of noise together with five Taoist elements (metal, wood, earth, fire and water), and the Chinese zodiac all relate to *fengshui*. When surveying the proposed site of any construction project, masters of geomancy take into account the local animal and plant life, subterranean caves and fault lines and the prevailing colors of the locality.

Each person's relationship with the elements is dictated by the year of their birth. Masters of *fengshui* will tell anyone born in a year of fire that too much of the water element — the color black, fountains or other artificial water sources at home — are inauspicious as water destroys fire. Positive features are the color green, plants and in particular a wooden dwelling as wood gives birth to fire. A fire element person should sleep in the southern part of their home.

Those born in an earth year should not have too many plants, but other fire elements bring luck because according to Chinese cosmology, fire gives birth to earth. It is best for people born under this element to sleep at the center of their house. As members of a family are likely to be born under different signs, the ruling element is that of the householder.

Compass points are also very important in *fengshui*. The North is associated with career; the Northeast with education, spirituality and intelligence; the East with masters of the family and the past; the Southeast with wealth and the South with fame. The Southwest is considered of great importance in social relationships and marriage, and the West for creativity, children and the future. The Northwest is of help when traveling. None, however, is associated with health. This may seem strange to Westerners, but within Chinese logic, good health depends on all aspects of a life, in particular harmonious relations with people and the environment.

The *fengshui* of a place is not immutable. In China it is generally believed that *fengshui* changes every 10 years. New elements in a landscape, like electric pylons, felled or planted trees, dried up creeks — all cause *fengshui* to change.

One person's good *fengshui* can be another's ruin, as people react differently to the earth's energy. When searching for solutions to per-

Upturned roofs are defense against evil spirits — they cannot go down to the earth because of such roofs.

Bending bridges and lotus ponds are indispensable attribute of the traditional Chinese garden, created with all *fengshui* requirements. Cheng Family Temple (Guangdong province).

sonal problems Westerners visit a psychoanalyst, whereas people in China prefer to consult a *fengshui* master. According to one famous exponent: "The right *fengshui* is like a good friend who helps make reaching a goal easier". Bad *fengshui*, on the other hand, is like a misguided advisor who creates obstacles to progress. Like many people, I believe each person has his or her own fate that eventually becomes obvious. Strokes of luck may seem to make life easier, but masters of *fengshui* are adamant that "Hard earned achievements bring more happiness than do easy gains." Who am I to disagree?

Magic Numbers

The last digit of my home phone number in Beijing is 4. "So what?" European readers might ask. This was my attitude when I first lived in China; I couldn't understand why Chinese friends were so shocked at my indifference to the number 4. But China brings new discoveries every day, and I have since seen the light. I know now that Chinese people have their own ways of preserving their well-being, and they see to avoiding the number 4 as a good way to stay safe.

Number 4 is pronounced *si* in Mandarin Chinese, similar to the word for death and is hence considered inauspicious. Hospital No.4 in Beijing was renamed recently because people were loath to take their ills to a place with such a "deadly" name. On the other hand, if you have never been to China before you will be surprised to find so many different goods priced at 168 yuan. Why? Ask your Chinese friend or guide and they will tell you that enunciation in sequence of the numbers 1, 6 and 8 brings happiness because *yao*, *liu* and *ba* sound very similar to *yaoliufa*, which means "the straight way to prosperity".

Every culture has its own lucky numbers and portents. Many of my compatriots consider 7 as lucky, but are wary of the number 13 and avoid it at all costs. In Western Christian culture 666 is synonymous of the Satan, but I have seen this figure written large as a street

address on buildings in Beijing and Shanghai. In China the numbers 6, 8 and 9 are considered auspicious, and mobile phone numbers that contain these three digits are much more costly than the others that don't.

Chinese numerology has its roots in Taoist traditions, and is clearly explained in the *Book of Changes*. According to customs, odd numbers symbolizes the bright male *yang*, and even numbers the dark undefined female *yin*.

Zero symbolizes non-existence, completeness and the godhead that, having no beginning or end, is eternal and also symbolized by a circle.

One represents honor, leadership and permanent development.

Two means to double, and is the number of cooperation and balance between *yin* and *yang*, man and woman. One popular Chinese saying is that "happiness comes as two." The character associated with weddings and engagements is *xi* written twice: double happiness.

Three makes everything possible. It is a number linked to luck and success. It is also a spiritual number, as according to the *Book of Changes*; three unites heaven, earth and man. When Chinese people go to a temple and make obeisance they kowtow three times.

Four represents temporal matters. Its foundation is the earth and its round roof is the heaven. Chinese people believe that this number strengthens the balance between heaven and earth.

Five is popular in Chinese culture because of its midway position between 1 and 9, and also because of five philosophical elements — water, metal, wood, fire and earth. There are also five blessings — longevity, prosperity, health, a virtuous life and natural death.

As I said before, the pronunciation of 6 in Chinese sounds similar to the word for prosperity and hence is a very lucky number.

Seven is a universally good number, and for several reasons in China.

Its pronunciation is similar to that for assurance, and Buddhists believe that there are seven reincarnations and seven weeks of mourning after a death. For centuries people in China have believed that the number 7 is an integral aspect of a woman's life. As they see it, at 7 months old a girl infant gets her first teeth, at age 7 her second teeth appear, at 14 — 7 doubled — she begins to menstruate, and at age 49 (7 squared) her reproductive years are generally over.

The word 8 in Chinese sounds similar to that for multiplication, and also wealth, and within *fengshui* the 8 trigrams (*bagua*) symbol in the *Book of Changes* symbolizes protection. As 7 regarded as significant for a woman, so 8 is of a great importance to a man. A boy gets his first teeth when he is 8 months old, loses and replaces them when he is 8 years old, at 16 he reaches maturity and at 64 (8 squared) his sexual power leaves him.

Nine is the best number because it contains characteristics of all the others. It is complete and needs no other digit to be perfect as it is the last stage of everything. To the ancient Chinese 9 was the largest number pertaining to human matters as ten and upward belong to Heaven. The number 9 was therefore solely for the Emperor's use, and if any court official was found to have 9 dragons embroidered on his robes he was immediately sentenced to death, along with all his family. There were 9,999.5 rooms in the Forbidden City and the line of knobs on any door — horizontal or vertical — number exactly 9.

I spent winter holidays in my home country Belarus. It was there that I realized how sensitive I have become to numbers, in the Chinese way of course. I now regard 7, 8 and 9 as my best friends. My Belarus mobile phone number has double 8 as two last digits (it is not that expensive to get it at home). The famous scientist Niles Bore once said about horseshoe: "It brings good luck even to those, who don't believe in its power". This saying explains best why Chinese influence has made me treat numbers with respect — just in case.

Affair with Colours

Long before the red color became associated in China at first with the Communist Party's banner and then with the national flag, the red had been the most beloved color of the Kingdom of Heaven. Over centuries the Chinese has associated this color with joy, happiness and everything good. It is widely believed to be auspicious and hence brides are dressed in red. New Year is symbolized by *chun lian* wishes written on red bands. Even traditional envelopes with money gifts for weddings and New Year — all envelopes are red! Yes, China has a long and happy affair with the red color. And this affair goes on and on. Nowadays gift envelopes are of the same red color and every New Year is greeted by plenty of red lanterns. At any day of the year every restaurant has red lanterns at its entrance. Every commodity in red package has more chances to be sold out than the very same item wrapped in any other color.

Forbidden City in Beijing.

Thereupon I am very lucky as the red color is my favorite since childhood. In my home country Belarus it is not easy to understand for many people my thirst for this bright flaming tint. Dressed in red from head to toe in China I look something common —

many people here wear dresses of the same color. Indeed, this country is home for the red.

Don't forget — in China nothing is in usual manner, everything has its explanation and deep-laid meaning often not recognizable from the first (especially foreigner's) sight. Therefore red and other colors loved by the Chinese didn't become such all of a sudden; every one has its history and particular sense.

A bird's eye view of Beijing offers a gaily colorful scene: magnificent imperial palaces with yellow-golden roofs, captivating flower gardens

Forbidden City in Beijing: yellow roofs and red walls. The color red means solemnity, wealth and honor, yellow — power and emperor.

dotted with green roofs and grey quarters nearby — plenty of one-storied buildings with grey walls and the same grey tiles....

In ancient China the color red meant solemnity, wealth and honor. Primitive human beings lived near Beijing 10,000-20,000 years ago left rock paintings in their caves. Guess, what is the dominant color of those paintings? Right you are — indeed, it is red. Red painted palaces appeared in China more than 2,000 years ago. Look at the Forbidden City with its red walls and yellow roofs — through them you can understand China better.

Looking at the imperial palaces it is easy to observe that the second important color is the yellow. After the red it is the second most important color of the Middle Kingdom, it meant power and emperor. It is the predominant color of the Forbidden City, magnificent residence which was the house of the Chinese emperors for around 500 years. Almost all its houses and other buildings are roofed with yellow glazed tiles. Why? For better understanding we have to go back to the notion of five elements. As we all remember, the ancient Chinese believed that the universe was made up of five elements: wood, fire, earth, metal and water. The most important element among the five was the earth which represents the centre. Yellow has long been considered the purest

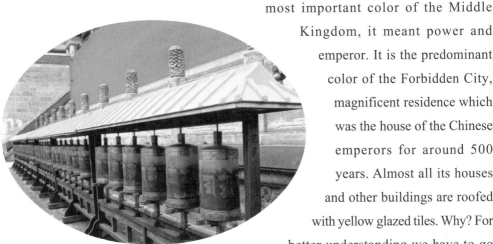

Eight temples of Chengde, Hebei Province is included in the UNESCO World Heritage list. Every one of them is an exact copy of original temples situated in different parts of the vast country. This one is a Tibetan Buddhism temple.

A corridor of Putuozong Temple, Chengde, Hebei Province.

among all colors, the color of earth. It symbolizes dignity and ritual. Very likely because of these reasons this color was loved by emperors — they were widely believed to be the world's supreme rulers.

The Tang (618-907) emperors and their family members adopted the practice of the previous Sui Dynasty (581-618), and wore robes made from yellow silk of special "imperial" tint. Others were not allowed to wear yellow dresses. It was how yellow became symbolic imperial color. People of the country regarded this color as a symbol of power.

By the way, in the remarkable Bernardo Bertolucci film *The Last Emperor* there is a scene directly connected to the importance of the color yellow. Young Pu Yi, already dethroned but not yet aware of this fact and still living in the Forbidden City, noticed that his play-

Chinese Customs and Wisdoms ▼

mate wears dress of that tint of the yellow reserved exclusively for the emperors. Only after this shocking discovery Pu Yi has realized that he is not the emperor any more, China is a republic and yellow is available for everybody to use and wear.

Yellow glazed-tile roofs were used in the Imperial Palace in the Song Dynasty (960-1279). It was stipulated in the Ming and Qing dynasties that the yellow glazed-tiles could be used exclusively by the emperors — on their palaces and tombs, or on temples built under the direct orders of the "sons of Heaven."

Any other person — official or his family members, let alone commoners — was forbidden to wear yellow or to use the color as decoration of

Red lanterns against the background of grey walls of the Chang Family mansion (Shanxi province).

interior or to live in a house decorated with a golden yellow roof. The price of transgression could be high: execution.

For surprise of many, there is a building in the Forbidden City with black, not yellow roof — namely, Wenyuange, the Imperial Library. But actually only those uninitiated are surprised. Contrary to them readers of this book already know the Five Elements theory. So, we know that the black color represents water, and water destroys fire. Thus the black roof of the library which contained a great many of highly inflammable books was a *fengshui* protection against fire.

Miao minority representatives during the tourism expo.

The Forbidden City aside there is another construction in Beijing with the same colors — red walls and yellow roofs: Yonghegong Temple (Palace of Harmony). This temple was the official mansion of Emperor Yongzheng (r. 1723-1735) from the Qing Dynasty — before he ascended the throne. After Yongzheng became the emperor, the complex stood empty because in accordance with the Chinese tradition, nobody, even members of the emperor's family, was allowed to live in the very same building which the emperor-to-be had once lived in. Yongzheng himself returned here only after his death — his corpse was carried to the mansion for mourning. In order to show respect towards the deceased monarch, the green-glazed tiles were replaced with yellow ones within 15 days. Though the Yonghegong turned into

Chinese football fans are real patriots carrying national flags for all matches with the China's team participation.

lamasery only in 1744, its yellow-glazed tiles demonstrate its affiliation to the imperial family for nearly 300 years.

Buildings in which royal princes lived were roofed with green-glazed tiles. At the order of ancient emperors, ordinary people, craftsmen, chefs and all others' houses had to be built in grey — both walls and roofs. It was the color of subjection, of those inferior.

Blue is the color of heaven and thus main buildings of the Temple of Heaven — by the way, it is the symbol of Beijing — were roofed with blue-glazed tiles.

Nowadays yellow and red are still the symbolic colors of China. They are the colors of the national flag. Chinese athletes are often dressed in red and yellow in international sport competitions.

China's affair with colors goes on.

Bells, Drums and Time Keepers

Conception of time is the holistic philosophical one, but at the same time it is a quite concrete one, we easily use it on a daily basis. Time is a continuing concern throughout Chinese history. One of the first responsibilities of any new dynasty was to regulate the calendar of the Kingdom of Heaven: if time were ever allowed to become disordered, the consequences would be dire.

The fundamental conception of time was already in place in the Shang Dynasty (1600-1046 BC). The basic unit of time (at least for most record-keeping purposes) was the day. Days were enumerated in a cycle of 60, produced by combining a set of ten "heavenly stems" (*tiangan*) with another set of twelve "earthly branches" (*dizhi*). This same cycle of 60 was later used to number consecutive years creating the full astrological cycle.

The 60-days cycle was divided into six weeks of ten days each. The moon was the basis of the month, actually the same word, *yue*, means both moon and month. Months alternated between long ones of 30 days and short months of 29 days to account for the 29.53-day mean period of a lunar cycle. Since this produced a year lasting only 354 days, it was necessary roughly every three years to add an extra month to bring the lunar year in line with the solar year. Echoes of these traditions can be felt these days: this is why the Chinese New Year fluctuates between late January and late February.

Nowadays Beijing as any other big city in China is filled with various sounds with automobile horns and bicycle bells rising above all others. This abundance of sounds creates unimaginable and unique cacophony that millions of people worldwide immediately associate with Asia. But long before these associations, entirely different sounds filled ancient Chinese

citie — and those of drums and bells were the most often to be heard. The instruments were used not only for entertainment. In ancient days, Beijing had a notion of "morning bell and evening drum" and during 652 years they were the main timetelling device for the people of the capital. All big cities of the Kingdom of Heaven had the same devices for the very same purposes. Bells and drums not only said to people what time it was but also told what to do during this particular hour.

The Drum Tower and the Bell Tower were built in 1272 in Beijing's Gulou especially for this loud "clock." They served as timepieces and

Candelabrum of 15 bronze lamps (Han Dynasty).

warning devices for the capital during the three dynasties — Yuan (1271-1368), Ming (1368-1644) and Qing (1644-1911). Fortunately they have survived to this day. Both towers have been destroyed by fires and then rebuilt several times over the years. In 1925 the Drum Tower was converted into a Beijing Popular Education Center and the neighboring Bell Tower into a cinema under the Education Center. After the People's Republic of China was established in 1949, special funds were allocated to restore the towers on a large scale. An automatic fire-extinguishing system was adopted to protect the wooden structures against fire, their main enemy. The towers were opened to the public in the 1980s as a place of historical interest and tourist attraction. Since 1990, the age-old bell in the Bell Tower regenerated its clock function by ringing on the Chinese New Year's Eve as part of the celebrations.

There used to be one big bell in the Bell Tower and 25 drums in the Drum Tower, a big drum in the centre surrounded by 24 little ones. The 24 surrounding drums symbolized the 24 solar terms in China's lunar calendar.

In accordance with the conception of twelve heavenly stems daily time consisted of a dozen hours, each lasting 120 minutes. The first hour of the Chinese day began at 23:00. Minutes and seconds were captured by a water-powered clock called a clepsydra.

During the Qing Dynasty, the bell boomed through Beijing 54 times a night preceded by an equal number of beats from the drum. How Beijingers managed to keep sleeping amidst such a roll is still a big mystery for me. In five separate two-hour intervals (*wugeng*) between the hours of 19:00 and 5:00, the bell was struck quickly 18 times, slowly 18 times, and then 18 more times neither slow nor fast in moderate tempo. Then the cadence was repeated once again for a total of 108 rings as 108 is the most auspicious Buddhist number (actually it is the number of beads of Buddha's rosary).

The first evening bell indicated *xu* hour (19:00-21:00) and spelled the end of the working day for the people of the city. The second period (*hai*, 21:00-23:00) indicated it was time to seal the city gates and to shut the transportation. The third (*zi*, 23:00-1:00) meant it was time for the emperor to prepare for the court; the fourth (*chou*, 1:00-3:00) summoned officials to the palace while the last (*yin*, 3:00-5:00) set served as the end of the imperial business.

The first morning bell was the one rung at *mao* hour — 5.00. It was a peculiar alarm clock for the townsfolk — the city gates were opened and a new day for the bustling capital was about to begin.

The tradition of striking the bell as a means of keeping time was carried on for more than a decade into the Republican era, and stopped in November 1924 when the last emperor Pu Yi left the Forbidden City.

Nowadays bells and drums are not used for time-telling any more — everybody can afford to own his/her own wrist-watch and set personal time for going to bed and to wake up. But in fact many old traditions are still alive and many Chinese today — exactly like centuries ago — go to bed early and get up also very early, often with sunrise. It is not rare to see people in parks and on streets at 6.00 doing morning exercises. It looks like that the "morning bell and evening drum" are in their blood.

One fifth of the world population lives in accordance with the Beijing

A man in the Small Goose Pagoda, Xi'an.

time. What is the time-telling device of today? In fact, Beijing time doesn't come from the capital, it comes from the Shaanxi Observatory in the northwest China. This observatory is operated by the Academy of Sciences.

The observatory's four 208-metre iron towers are surrounded by guards and high walls. Before 1949, Chinese time relied on the United States Navy Observatory. In the early 1950s, China's time service was provided by the Shanghai Astronomical Observatory but due to inadequate equipment, and an unsuitable geographical position — Shanghai is too far east of the centre of the country — the time service was not accurate. Mao Zedong said that China must have its own standard time. On March 26, 1966 the decision was approved to set up China's stan-

Pudong New Area of Shanghai. Many People think that this panoramic view is more beautiful than New York's Manhattan.

dard-time service centre. Project 326 began and the number eventually became the code number for the time-service centre which started providing standard Beijing time on December 15, 1970. China Central Television Station and Central People's Broadcasting Station adjust their clocks according to the standard time frequency reported by the Pucheng Time Service Centre, and they provide the people of Beijing and the whole country with the correct time. Despite the fact that China actually stretches for five time zones, the official time in any corner of the country is the same, that of Beijing.

Bells and drums are long gone, now scientists in white smocks are the main keepers of the Chinese time.

Boxing that Bruce Lee Turned into an Art

Do you like Bruce Lee and his furious fists? You are not alone; he was also the Gods' favorite. After his early death Bruce Lee became a legend. Many youngsters haven't even seen his movies but know for sure that all present heroes — induding Jacky Chang — are somehow his students. Recent film *Crouching Tiger, Hiding Dragon* started another huge wave of interest to Chinese martial arts. By the way, in China this movie was not a big hit at all. Frankly, I was also not impressed although reconstruction of the old Beijing in the movie is excellent. The reason why I am so unanimous with the Chinese is simple: local TV stations. *Kungfu* movies are very popular here and every night there is a choice of 2-3 films with all necessary attributes as furious fights, flights over roofs, love and hate. Indeed, it is very difficult to surprise the Chinese with a movie of this genre.

Bruce Li

People around the world are more and more dragged into amazing *wushu* world. But martial arts specialist is not only the person making blazing strikes; it is also the person with knowledge of Chinese traditions and culture, as it is the usual context in which martial arts exist. That is why outside of China martial arts in many cases are just adults' favorite game.

Different martial art forms suit to different people depending on the type of person and the person's targets. For example, if you want to be flexible and quick and to strike beautifully and gracefully probably Long Fist is your martial art form. But if your aim is to practice for many years to come and to stay strong and relaxed, your choice should be likely *taijiquan*. Another important factor to take into account is your body and its abilities, the Chinese are sure that different boxing styles correspond to different physical types. If you are not created for the Long Fist you will never be perfect in this style even if practicing every day. Yes, it sounds a bit fatalistic but this is China: find what suits you best and don't constrain your nature.

A Shaolin monk practices Shaolin *kungfu*.

Popularity of the Chinese *wushu* as well as other martial arts around the world decreased drastically in the epoch of firearms. It doesn't matter what boxing style you fight and how often you practice — a bullet is faster. People in China know that too and thus martial arts here first of all are body

Shaolin Monastery in Henan Province is famous not only for its martial arts but for Pagoda Forest as well.

Shaolin monks.

abilities' training, self-defense, health strengthening and — important aspect — preservation of the traditional culture. After all *wushu* involves many principles of eastern traditio — philosophy, religion, medicine and of course military practice.

For example *taijiquan* movements reflect philosophical ideas of *yin* and *yang*. It unites theory of five cosmological elements and principles of *bagua* (eight trigrams) with certain positions and creates continuous flow of motion. Shaolin boxing originated from the famous monastery of the same name in Henan Province. It was strongly influenced by Buddhist philosophy mixed with Indian yoga. It is accepted that the founder of this boxing style was legendary monk Boddhitharma who came to China in the 6th century in search of nirvana. Did he find it — nobody knows, but for many centuries Boddhitharma legend is an essential part of the Shaolin Monastery.

The Chinese say that "every city has its own dialect and every region has its own *wushu* style." Very often the difference is minor but the most well-known is that the North styles pay special attention to leg strikes and those developed in the South — to fist technique. If you have long legs then Northern styles *cha quan* and *hua quan* are a real boon for you. If you are stocky and lissome then go for the Southern styles *mo jia quan* and *chai li fo*. However bear in mind that the Southern styles demand strong knees for low and long stances. It is a style for enduring people.

The aim of almost all *wushu* styles is a strong body. If training aims at development of strong muscles and physical endurance then the "eternal system," *wai jia quan,* is used. "Inner system," *nei jia quan*, accentuates on breathing technique, slow circular movements and development of *qi* energy. For centuries specialists argued which one of these schools was the most effective. In fact, "eternal system" on a certain stage

Students of martial arts schools around the Shaolin Monastery recite classical texts of Chinese philosophers.

borrows exercises of the "inner system" and vice versa. It depends on aims of the practitioner. The "eternal" styles are best fit for those attracted by fighting, speed and strikes. The "inner" ones are for people concentrating on spiritual side of exercises. It can come as a surprise but specialists affirm that "eternal" styles are easier to perfect especially if you are physically strong. Practicing of "inner" styles demands patience, endurance and discipline. Classical "inner" system very popular around China is *taijiquan* as well as *xingyi quan* and *bagua zhang*.

Legendary times when every *kungfu* master chose his disciples are long gone. Now in most cases there are students who choose their tutor depending on his reputation, aims and — last but not least — on their financial abilities.

Dreamed about Shaolin for all these years? No problems — enroll and study. The monastery was built in 498 and was well-known China's *wushu* centre during the Northern Wei Dynasty (386-534). But it is Hong Kong movies of 1970s that made its martial arts Mecca reputation. Since then life in Shaolin has changed forever. Just 16 years ago there was not a single hotel in the vicinity but nowadays there are plenty of hotels and around 50 martial arts schools with more than 50,000 students.

Every morning, schools start in the same way: getting up at 5 o'clock in the morning, endless run in a school yard, covering a field with floor-mats (in every season training is outdoors), slow *taijiquan* movements and only then students practice what most of us imagine when thinking of Shaolin — blazing strikes, fast movements and miracles of flexibility. Among all exercises the most impressive are undoubtedly those of *sanda* form — this is boxing style allowing full contact of fighters. And don't expect typical monk's dress — it is reserved for performances and competitions.

The most popular martial art around the world is admittedly *taijiquan* which is practiced in China by millions till very advanced age. It is a real treasure for one wishing to stay flexible; maintain good circulation of the blood and well-balanced organism. Cultivation of *qi*, energy used for both self-treatment and fighting, makes up a big part of training.

One of the best-known *taijiquan* forms is Yang family style which in its simplified form is not that difficult. Other styles, for example Chen family style, demand more efforts: its positions are painfully slow with high pushes, so it needs special flexibility. Chen style is popular with youth and it is this style highly cultivated in Shaolin — slow movements and blazing strikes. Among others not that famous styles are Sun and Wu.

"Pushing hands" is one of the main exercises in *taijiquan*, Chen family style. On the right is Chen Ziqiang, member of Chen family in 13th generation.

Taijiquan exercises include "pushing hands" and others. "Pushing hands" teach how to react correctly to a rival's movements. Good understanding and adequate reaction is the main weapon for fighters. They are purposefully taught cheating the enemy pretending to concede because it is easier to control and redirect the force while retreating. Mastering of all nuances of *taiji* is great art requiring efforts and years of training.

Wing chun boxing was invented by Buddhist monk Ng Mui

who passed his skills to Wing Chun. It is fierce and dynamic system promising fast results for novices. This is the Bruce Lee style. The main feature in *wing chun* is speed, the main methods — deviations, tricks and fast kicks. Positions are simple and straight, very different from other styles.

Everyday routine practice in the Tagou Martial Arts School near Shaolin Monastery.

Wing chun based on the "central line theory." It draws imaginary line along the centre of a human's body from head to heel and strikes along this line. It passes through the most sensitive points: eyes, nose, lips, mouth, throat, heart, solar plexus and groin. Every strike at any of these points weakens the opponent and potentially is very dangerous. While blocking somebody else's strikes hands don't stray beyond the width of the shoulders which is the limit of any possible attacks. It is exactly why *wing chun* looks so simple. The punch takes its strength from shoulders, elbows and wrists. They are delivered with high speed along the shortest distance between the boxers. Routine paired exercises are called *chi sau*; they teach how to remain soft and even a bit pliable responding to attacks. Softness develops relaxation and gives speed in counter-attacking.

Bagua zhang is translated as "eight-trigram boxing." This is one of the strangest martial art styles to witness. *Bagua* boxers are feared for fury and untraditional moves. *Bagua* practitioner revolves in imaginary circle changing speed and direction and occasionally thrusting out a palm strike. Inspiration for this style can be found in eight trigrams (an arrangement of three broken and unbroken lines) of the *Book of Changes*. The trigrams are often arranged in the form of a circle, hence the fighter's movements.

The main skills in this kind of boxing are wiles, tricks, speed and unpredictability. Force usually is not met with force but deflected by circular movements. Another trade mark of this style is using the palm not the fist as the main striking weapon.

Art of *bagua zhang* is deeply esoteric and virtually off-limits for non-Chinese. There are not many real teachers left.

Xingyi quan is another soft, "inner" boxing style. Like *taijiquan,* trainings emphasize development of *qi* energy, however moves of *xingyi* are more dynamic and powerful. Philosophy behind this style is not passive which differs

from that of *taiji*.

Some people think that *xingyi quan* is the oldest martial art of China. It is this style that imitates movements of 12 animals comprising Chinese zodiac. There are different schools with different techniques but standard forms of *xingyi quan* include schools of dragon, tiger, horse, monkey, chicken, harrier, Chinese ostrich, swallow, eagle, bear, water lizard and snake. It is a must to understand the spirit of each animal through its form, idea and intentions. All these animals enjoy their special place in Chinese culture and traditions.

Before studying the animal forms, students must start with five punches which are blocking system of *xingyi quan*. Strikes are taught one after another until perfected. Every strike symbolizes one of five elements of the Chinese philosophy — metal, wood, water, fire and earth. The punches reflect cycle of conquest and creation that reveal itself in interaction of the elements.

Xingyi is performed in a relaxed state, emphasizing calm but observant mind. Movements are quick and direct, the body unites as a whole while targeting. Training is a difficult and tiresome task; it consists of many postures that must be held for a long time to develop *qi*. Force is met with force and not with tricks and deviations like in other systems. Like with *bagua zhang* it is difficult to find a good teacher of *xingyi quan* and they are often very secretive. Yes, Bruce Lee is not born every day.

Chinese practice *taijiquan* even in advanced age.

There are plenty of martial art forms and styles in China with every single one of them having its own philosophy and spirit. Every one is the distillation of boxers' experience and the direct connection to centuries-old traditions. You will never be a winner fighting only with arms and legs. It is the spirit conquering all obstacles and throwing enemies.

The Centuries-old Dream of Flight

A sky densely dotted by kites is one of China's most joyful sights. As you approach Tiananmen Square and observe colored dots among the clouds you might feel puzzled as to what exactly is going on. Then you see the people holding silk strings, faces upturned, and everything is explained: you have come upon a great day for kite flying.

There are dozens of stories as to how the kite was first invented. My personal favorite tells of a peasant wearing a large bamboo hat as he worked in the field. Suddenly a strong gust blew his hat off. He ran after it but was only able to catch the hat string. After running along for sometime, holding the string as the hat flew high overhead, he suddenly realized how much fun he was having with his flying bamboo hat. This was how the first kite was born.

According to another legend, the artisans' patron Gongshu Ban and philosopher Mo Di (?-380 BC) made kites shaped like birds that flew and somersaulted for three days in a row. Although kite-flying is generally a leisure pursuit, during China's long history kites were also used for military purposes. They would sometimes be loaded with gunpowder to blow up an enemy camp, and were also used for dropping leaflets. This was the method used in 1232 to encourage prisoners of war captured by Mongols to raise a rebellion.

Resourceful Chinese also adapted kites for fishing by attaching line, hook and bait to a kite and sending it out to the middle of a lake or a river.

During the 7th-8th century the Chinese invented musical kites that whistled, groaned and emitted harp-like sounds.

Ancient Chinese philosophers loved kites, although it is not immediately obvious what kites and philosophy have in common. In traditional China there was never a worthwhile deed or invention that did not merit some degree of philosophical insight. To early Taoists, kite-flying was a meditative exercise. Watching the

soaring flight of a man-made object evoked images of the Supreme Way, and the slightest breath was associated with a flight of imagination.

Chinese kites are genuine works of art in amazing designs. Among them are multi-colored carps and butterflies, eagles and snails, peacocks and bats, heroes of famous literary works and Peking Opera masks, and gods and dragons, to name just a few. Modern times have also

Dragon kite consists of many layers, its length can reach 100 m. To fly such kite is real art.

During the Kite Festival in Weifang (Shandong Province) one can see kites of various forms.

paid their aerial tribute and there are kites in the shape of tractors, famous buildings or favorite basketball teams.

Over the centuries *fengzheng* (kite in Chinese) has developed into various types: kite in the shape of a dragon, kite with flexible or fixed wings, in the form of a box, etc. They also vary in size, from very big, to big, medium, small and miniature. Small ones are most popular today for their speed and durability. Many Chinese cities are famous for a particular type of kite. Tianjin, for example, specializes in soft wings, while Weifang is known for its long multi-layered dragons.

Chinese believe that kite flying is good for health and that flying *fengzheng* in spring banishes excessive internal heat and strengthens immunity. Even watching kite flying is beneficial as it is good exercise for the cervical vertebrae and eyesight.

It is best for two people to fly a kite: one to hold the reel and the other to fly kite itself. A big dragon kite needs three at least: one to hold a reel and kite head, another to support the section and a third for the tail. Big dragons are sometimes as long as 100 meters.

"When you feel a gust approach, just free your kite and let it fly," says Beijinger Wang Jingfen, to whom kite flying in Tiananmen Square is a favorite pastime. She makes it look supremely easy, but I know from experience that it is far less simple than it looks, especially for beginners. You need skill and experience to be good kite flyer. Like everything else, it requires skill too.

Tiananmen Square is the most popular place in Beijing and the whole of China to fly *fengzheng*. Flyers and spectators meet here to admire kites and share experience. It is where foreigners first encounter traditional kites, but there are kites enthusiasts in any Chinese park.

Creating kites is a traditional Chinese art that demands concentration, craftsmanship and inspiration. The first step is design. A pattern is drawn directly on to a length of silk, and the slightest hesitation or hand tremor ruins the fabric. This is how you can distinguish a real master — he draws a perfect pattern at the first attempt. A bamboo frame is placed over the design and excess fabric cut away. A string is then attached to the kite "body."

To some degree kites are an actualization of the ancient dream of flying, enacted in the opening scene of one of my favorite movies, *Andrey Rublev* by Andrey Tarkovsky. A man equipped with wooden

Kite Festival in Weifang (Shandong Province)

wings resembling a hang-glider flies from a medieval church belfry shouting ecstatically: "I am flying! I am flying!" His rapid and fatal landing does not matter because to this man who dares to make his dream come true, his few seconds of flight are worth more than life itself.

In the West we say that a man flies like a bird, while the Chinese think of a dragon in flight. It first gathered speed, using clouds as a springboard, and after reaching a height of 40 *li* uses blasts of air to take him in a free soar.

Doesn't that sound like hang-gliding, where it is possible to glide through the sky using air currents? And doesn't a hang-glider resemble a huge kite?

The first mention of a flying machine capable of carrying a man is found in chronicles of the Northern Qi Dynasty (550-577). Researchers are sure that the first flight on a device resembling a modern hang-glider occurred in China in AD 559, exactly 1335 years before Baden-Powell in Europe.

Before 1910, all books on aviation had an opening chapter on kites, and early airmen referred to their airplanes as kites. In the Aeronautics Museum in Washington, USA, I noted the *fengzheng* was described as the "first man-made flying object."

When I see senior citizens happily flying their kites I feel assured that true traditions never die.

Blossoming Virtues

When entering Chinese parks and gardens, a visitor is immediately captured by their Oriental charms. In such parks everything slows down including time which seems to have become viscous sugar syrup. It is not easy to understand how much time you have spent here — an hour or a century, and in fact it doesn't matter because your only dream is to stay there forever, sitting in an open pavilion,

Wangshi Garden, Suzhou.

admiring blossoming peaches, playing *erhu* (Chinese fiddle), sipping green tea from an almost transparent porcelain cup, envying lazy colorful fish swimming in a pond. Gardens in the Kingdom of Heaven are nothing of the kind we have in Europe, they are miniature and exquisite, meandering and significant, elegant and not fussy. It is hardly believable that all landscapes in such parks are not natural but man-made, created by famous gardeners getting inspiration from the eternal search — how to mirror human nature in stones' shadows and paths' curves. Every element of such garden has a mark of century-old culture and traditions.

China is paradise for aesthetes whose refined souls are so sensitive to beauty of things and events. The Kingdom of Heaven has a long tradition of admiring flowering plants, special festivals are held to enjoy beauty of blooming peonies, peaches and *meihua* plum. During the autumn's Double Ninth Festival people gather in gardens and parks to admire beautiful chrysanthemums. The Chinese are very sensitive to plants' beauty, they endow flowers and other plants with special virtues and are able to see the best human features in interlace of petals.

Chinese truly adore blossoming peaches.

In great antiquity, however, people had a different, very pragmatic, attitude towards plants, studying and growing them in medical purposes. At that time the first catalogues of medicinal herbs, flowers and trees appeared. Famous scientist of the 16th century Li Shizhen in his book described characteristics of 1, 100 plants.

Later on the tradition of decorative plants growing appeared. The Chinese gardeners could always give an explanation why the best sorts of fruit trees or the most beautiful flowers grow in this or that particular area. They are sure that the main reason for that is abundant "energy of Heaven and Earth." Well-known scientist of the 11th century Ouyang Xu said that harmonious combination of vital energies gave birth to "ordinary" plants, and lack of any vital forces produced surprisingly beautiful or vice versa — ugly specimen. If it was Heaven that went counter to natural order, freak of nature was born. If it was Earth that deviated from the natural order, something marvelous appeared.

Among all noble trees the Chinese regard the pine to be the best; it is symbol of straightforwardness and firmness. Gardener of the 17th century Wen Zhenheng advised to plant the pine in front of a study's windows, then placed a decorative

Bamboo and Bird by Song-dynasty artist Wu Bin. Bamboo is a favorite theme of Chinese astists.

Bamboo is very popular in China, it is symbol of straightforwardness and firmness.

stone over the roots and planted narcissuses, orchids and grasses around the tree. "Mountain pines are better to be planted in firm soil," Wen Zhenheng affirmed, "Its bark is like the Dragon's scales, the wind singing at its crown. Why leave the house for mountain peaks or for a sea shore?"

Another very popular plant is bamboo — resilient and coreless, embodiment of life-giving emptiness. The first book about bamboo appeared in China in the 5th century, according to which, gardeners were able to tell the difference between 300 bamboo varieties.

Every Chinese garden has "plants of happiness" in it, namely plum and peach, and in almost every park willows incline. They are said to represent the vital *yang* principle. In the south of the country magnolias and banana are planted everywhere bestowing beneficial shadow during summer, while in winter mandarin trees give out an exquisite aroma.

Peony.

In all centuries connoisseurs regarded peony as the "king of flowers," it was personification of pure *yang*. Luoyang City in Henan Province is famous for its splendid peonies since the Middle Ages. Every year the city hosts the Peony Festival attended by flower-lovers from all over the world. As early as in the 12th century, there were around 200 sorts of peonies known in China. "Dancing Lion Cub" peony with pastel colored petals, leaves resembling "jasper butterflies" and seeds like the "Golden Pavilion" was regarded as the best of them all.

Yin principle of the flower garden was represented by chrysanthemum, the most beautiful autumn flower, symbol of tranquility and longevity as well as heartfelt purity of a noble person. Among chrysanthemums the ones with petals resembling "multi-colored heron's feathers" are the most admired.

Hydrangeas, roses, narcissuses, camellias, hyacinths, pomegranates and orchids are also widely grown in China. Many roses popular these days in Europe actually originated from China.

This chrysanthemum is depicted on a decorative screen in the Chang Family mansion (Shanxi Province).

Among aquatic flowers the most popular is lotus, the main flower of Buddhism. According to a legend, Buddha himself was born inside a lotus. Of course, it is not without explanation: a lotus' stems reaching out of dark water depth towards the Sun run symbolically through all levels of the Universe and personify irrepressible force of nature. Its beautiful and delicate flowers blossoming over water surface symbolize a pure soul.

Lotuses in Chinese parks are firstly grown in special water tanks and only then are transplanted into ponds taking into consideration particular features of a local landscape. There are special rules for aquatic flowers: lotuses are planted a little farther from a bank, and nearer to a bank

or to a bridge water-lilies are planted. It is widely believed that water-lily with its small leaves and flowers are better admired from the short distance.

Ornamental plants and flowers are not only feast for eyes but also imbued with deep philosophical implication. Trees and flowers in the Chinese garden are not only images of eternal beauty, they also attempt to snatch and capture a single moment and its mood. In one household management book published during the Ming Dynasty (1368-1644), it was written: "A flower is grown during a whole year but admired in just 10 days".

Every Chinese garden has special corners to be visited in different seasons. "Winter" landscapes are composed of pines and frost-resisting plants and flowers; "spring" ones a riot of cherries, honeysuckle, almonds, early roses, violets and narcissuses. In "summer" corners of the garden, summer plants and broad-leaf trees such as oaks, ashes, beeches and platans are grown. In autumn season, people enjoy sweet smell of mandarin trees and beauty of chrysanthemums.

Centuries ago special rules for admiring plants in the garden were formulated. According to these rules, it was widely believed that the winter flowers were better to be enjoyed after the first snowfall when the sky cleared up. It was recommended to enjoy them as one sat in a secluded house. Flowers of spring had to

Plum Blossoms and Turtledove by Song-dynasty artist Zhao Ji.

be contemplated in sunlight when one sat on a terrace of an imposing palace during a cool day. It was believed that summer flowers were in their best after the rain, in fresh breeze, in the shadow of a branchy tree, in a bamboo grove or on a bank of a stream. Autumn flowers looked better in rays of sunset, in the gloaming, as one sat near front steps, on a mossy path or under twisted liana.

The most popular plants, both trees and flowers, were not only flora representatives, but also had many associations connected to them. For example, a pine evoked an image of sky-rocketing tree on a mountain slope and its mighty roots tearing up stony soil. Willow was associated with a water flow, bamboo — with a picture of lambent shadows during summer night, banana tree — with the sound of rain in dense foliage.

Lotus is the main flower of Buddhism, its flowers over the water represent heart purity in a "world of dust and filth."

Flowers, like any other things for contemplation, were imagined by the Chinese in a proper company. Every noble flower had its companions among lower-ranked flowers that reflected hierarchy peculiar to the Chinese way of thinking. Dog-roses and roses were regarded as the best companions for majestic peony, for white peony there were poppy and althaea, plum was accompanied by camellia and magnolia, lotus by tuberose, chrysanthemum by begonia.

There are direct parallels between flower kingdom and human's moral qualities. Orchid symbolizes elegancy and modesty, bamboo — straightforwardness and firmness, chrysanthemum — nobility in harsh times, magnolia — feminine beauty, lotus — heart purity in a "world of dust and filth"; happy married couple is often described as "two lotus flowers on one stem." Plum is regarded as symbol of longevity and happy marriage, persimmon — as joy of life and pomegranate as abundant posterity; it is widely believed in China that the more children in a family the happier it is. Poets regard *meihua* plum, peony, lotus and chrysanthemum as "four noble beings." Combination of plum with bamboo symbolizes lasting friendship and, together with a pine, three of them make the image of mutual devotion even in winter hard frost, and also the symbol of unity of the China's three main teachings: that of Confucianism (pine), Buddhism (bamboo) and Taoism (plum).

Bygone Feminine Allure

Though very rare but it is still possible to meet them — very old women with extremely small feet. They walk slightly staggering, depending on a stick or rather two, stopping to have a short rest quite often. With every passing day, the number of such elderly women with small feet grows less and less. Very soon 90-100 years old women with small feet will become history, so with the millennial tradition of binding feet, unique to China.

As legend has it, the first person to bind her feet for getting half-moon shape of them was Yao Niang, beloved wife of Emperor Li Yu of the Tang Dynasty (618-907). Li Yu ordered to build a stage in the shape of a lotus flower for Yao Niang. She was dancing on the stage with her feet bound. It became fashionable and soon ladies of the court followed suit.

Some historians doubt this version and believe that the practice of binding feet appeared for the first time during the Song Dynasty (960-1279). For my opinion, timing in this case is not that important: feet have been bound for thousands of years.

The tradition was started by ladies of noble and rich families and then it spread all over the country. Soon it became not just a fashionable trend but cruel necessity and indispensable attribute for every beautiful girl. Small feet became the most intimate and sexually attractive part of the woman's body, symbol of feminity. A girl with properly bound feet had the best chances for good marriage. Even a prostitute with small feet attracted wealthier clients.

Classical phrase of seven characters describes the ideal woman's foot: "slim, small, sharp, curved, fragrant, soft, and symmetric." Such foot was named "golden lotus" (*jinlian*), the ideal "lotus" was 10 cm in length. In medieval China rich men drank their wine from glasses shaped like a woman's shoe, therefore named "the golden lotus glass," *jinlian bei*.

Many researchers think, however, that the main reason for binding feet was not pursuit of beauty but much more prosaic reason — men's will to retain a woman at home and to limit her communication with the outside world. If this is the case, men proved to be right: it is not easy to move on such feet indeed. Most likely this tradition was introduced by Confucians who believed that the best place for a woman was her house and the only destination was to give birth. This had nothing to do with feet length. But extramarital affair was next to impossible to start.

A woman with small feet was considered very erotic. The Chinese thought that step of such a woman was extremely tempting as she had to balance rhythmically swinging her hips. Such walk inevitably caused pelvis anomalies (constriction and permanent exertion of muscular system) which in turn were very handy for men looking for sexual pleasures.

So, how did women get their "golden lotuses"? When a girl was 4 years old, four fingers of each of her feet were bent under and tied firmly to the foot. The bandages had to

Nowadays women with bounded feet are a big rarity. All of them are in very advanced age.

be changed from time to time, and her feet stopped growing. For getting the ideal "golden lotus," it was important to start binding at this age. Starting earlier — a girl might not survive pain and could stop walking at all; starting later — a foot was practically already formed and binding would not be effective. It was in this tender age the Chinese girls got to know that beauty demanded sacrifices and in some cases even physical sufferings. Only 4-5 years later sharp painful feeling blunted. But bear in mind: feet's binding was a life-long business. And during all their lives women felt even if dull but aches which disappeared only for short minutes when bandages were removed for washing and nails clipping. Then — hobbled again.

Binding deprived women of some popular pleasures, they stopped dancing. Since the Song Dynasty there were many famous singers and musicians among Chinese beauties and courtesans but no dancers.

Movements for liberation of

women in every country have their own national specifics. In China it was the wide movement against binding feet launched during decline of the Qing Dynasty (1644-1911) and widely developed during the first years of the Republic. By the way, Manchurians ruling in China under the name of the Qing Dynasty didn't bind their girls, so it was easy to tell Manchu from Han females — just casting a glance at their feet.

But the tradition of binding feet was dying out hard. It was wide spread in the countryside even in the first years after the New China was proclaimed in 1949. It is still possible to meet old ladies with the "golden lotuses" just slightly over 70 years old in villages.

It was not just the "golden lotuses" to define a feminine beauty. A slim girl possessing long fingers and soft palms, fine brows and small rosebud mouth — it is a portrait of the classical Chinese beauty. Ladies from noble families shaved off hairs on their forehead to visually lengthen face oval and tried to get an ideal lips contour by applying a lipstick roundly.

Hairs were arranged in complicated wavy coiffure with the help of pins. Experts compared such hair-styles to noble flowers or to "the dragon frolicking in the clouds." For best looks, noble women covered their faces with rice powder, cheeks with rouge and lips with a "ripe cherry" colored lipstick.

Some other adornments widely used were also very

popular — earrings, decorative pins and combs, rings and bracelets. Chinese beauties used floral water and fragrant soap and spent plenty of time sitting beside censers imbuing their clothes with aroma of incenses.

The face of a woman should always be dispassionate and her movements reserved and smooth, at least it was what etiquette demanded. To expose teeth when laughing was a sign of bad breeding. Echo of this belief can be easily seen in today's China as many local girls cover their mouth with a hand when laughing.

The Chinese are great philosophers, believing in deep connection between a body and a soul. A beautiful woman was not simply the one possessing "the golden lotuses" but the one able to keep up the conversation on painting and poetry. The Chinese believed (and still do) that one of the most important merits of every woman was her charm which has been described as the magic power of beauty hidden under cover of obedience.

The writer Li Yu believed that the secret of female charms was "in making old looking younger, ugly — more beautiful, usual — really amazing." Every woman's ability to be charming and fascinating "emanated from Heaven;" it can be understood only by intuition and can not be inherited. This elusive and fine substance doesn't disappear after a number of years and a charming woman always remains beautiful.

In multinational China, concepts of beauty are different for different ethnic groups. In the 17th century, Manchu males, founders of the Qing Dynasty, were captured by beauty of Han women and for the next two centuries married and took as concubines mostly Hans. It was only in the second half of the 19th century when one Manchu woman amazed the Emperor Xianfeng with her unusual beauty. Oval face, tall stature and loud voice of Ci Xi were in sharp contrast with other concubines of the Emperor's harem. Making her way from a concubine to the Empress, this "Little Orchid" (the name she was given at birth) ruled the huge country for many years. The richest monarchs of the world envied splendor of her court. For long years, the Empress managed to stay young-looking and attractive.

Foreigners visit Tibet for the first time have been astonished seeing beautiful local women — dark-complexioned with kingly bearing, long black hairs tied by black and red threads. But aroma-sensitive European men could hardly withstand specific "aroma" of rank melted butter which was usual smell for females living in this Roof of the World. Well, beauty is important but don't forget the climate! Unfavorable natural conditions have inevitably affected methods used by the Tibetan women to keep their appearance. Because of rarefied air, permanent winds, burning sun and unavoidable dryness, the women grease themselves so as to prevent weather skin and burns. They oil their faces with butter and then sprinkled with earth.

Girls of the Li minority living on the subtropical Hainan Island from of old cover their bodies with tattoos. Ancient legend tells that once a chieftain abused a beautiful girl and since then all females of the tribe tattooed their body, neck and legs making themselves look ugly and thus escaping the same fate. Nowadays it is very likely Li girls would be regarded as very stylish and beautiful in London or New York, don't you think?

After 1949, women Communists refused everything feminine, trading dresses for Mao Zedong trouser suits, splendid coiffures for short practical haircuts and throwing away all bourgeois doings such as powder, rouge and lipsticks. At that time women first of all became the Communism-constructors, everything else was secondary.

Tibetan women on their way to a festive party.

Reforms and opening-up policy declared by Deng Xiaoping in 1978 affected women's faces. Cosmetic business nowadays is one of the most flourishing industries with mushrooming beauty shops. Plastic surgery is in vogue, the most popular operation is double-fold eyelids, nose enhancement, breasts enlargement, wrinkles reduction and liposuction. The biggest group of plastic surgeons' clients is aged 20-40 but media have reported about 60+ clients. Most parents support their daughters' desires, believing that good looks increase chances for employment and marrying a well-to-do husband. Chinese women have proved that it is possible to build Communism and stay feminine at the same time. Well-done, ladies!

Soft as Silk

Statue of the great weaver Huang Dao Po of the Yuan Dynasty.

Clothing is a facet of Chinese tradition very much alive in the contemporary world. The milling streets and sidewalks of Beijing are peppered with people wearing classically cut Chinese jackets, infants dressed as little emperors, and elders who feel younger in the fashions of their youth. Those inspired to dress this way are, upon entering the clothing section of any department store, immediately engulfed in a sea of Chinese garments in updated styles and thousands of colors. The common feature of Chinese traditional wear is its fabric — all garments are made from silk.

According to Chinese legend, it was Leizu, wife of the legendary Yellow Emperor that first unraveled a silk cocoon. It dropped into her cup of tea on a summer day in 2640 BC as she rested under a mulberry tree. In the following 3,000 years, silk worms were one of the Middle Kingdom's most heavily guarded secrets.

In AD 300, a Chinese princess smuggled a silkworm out of the country. It was this treasured dowry item that brought the secrets of silk industry to the rest of the world, at least as legend would have it.

In any event, silk has always been valuable in China. In the Han (206 BC-AD 220) and Tang (618-907) dynasties, it was used

Silk with a motif of phoenix.

as currency. Peasants paid their taxes in grain and silk, and officials and members of society's upper echelons were awarded length of silk as a mark of their station.

Silk was the fabric of emperors, their wives, concubines and eunuchs; their everyday as well as ceremonial dress was fashioned from it. But emperor's silk garments had exclusive features. Their robes were made from exquisite Yun brocade, a work art in itself. This gorgeous fabric was woven silk, gold and silver thread intertwined with plumage of as many as 100 birds. It could only be hand woven, so just one length took years to complete. It took 13 years to weave the fabric for just one of Ming-dynasty (1368-1644)

Silk processing.

Yun Brocade Institute in Nanjing (Jiangsu Province). Today it is the only place in the country producing this gorgeous and likely the world most expensive fabric.

Emperor Wanli's ceremonial robes.

During the Qing Dynasty (1644-1911) all Yun brocade was sent to the Forbidden City. Some was used to make robes for the emperor and empress, and the rest was for clothes presented by the Son of Heaven to his favorite concubines and higher courtiers. A gift of Yun brocade was the ultimate honor and a family treasure that passed from generation to generation.

The honor of wearing Yun brocade having been confined to bygone Sons of Heaven and their intimates; it is not part of the universal image of Chinese clothing.

So what is? When thinking about Japan in this context, it is the kimono that springs to mind, while the mention of India conjures up the quintessentially feminine sari. And China? In all probability the image of a gracefully slender woman in a *qipao* (or *cheongsam* as it is called in the South) of richly embroidered lustrous silk or satin. The *qipao* is a relatively recent fashion. Its literal meaning "banner dress" refers to the gowns worn by Manchu women of the Banner clans — army regiments of the prospective Qing Dynasty. Upon establishment of the Qing in 1644, the dress also became fashionable among Han women.

The *qipao*'s heyday came in the 1920s-1930s. By this time it had changed dramatically in style, from wide and knee length to long and figure-hugging, with daringly high side slits. During the "cultural revolution" (1966-1976), *qipao* was, along with fur coats and high heels, considered "bourgeois;" women were well advised to exchange their sinuous silks for the blue cotton trousers and jacket known in the West as the "Mao suit," and in China, as the "Sun Yat-sen suit."

A Suzhou girl in silk *qipao* telling a story combined with singing to the accompany of a Chinese fiddle.

Qipao is in vogue once more in China and elsewhere as more and more European women are charmed by the way it flatters every figure. Cinema has also played its role in the resurgence of *qipao* popularity. In Cannes Film Festival award-winning movie *In the Mood for Love*, actress Maggie Cheung wears 20 different *qipao* and looks stunning in all of them.

Apart from the "cultural revolution" decade, women of China have never stopped wearing traditional clothes. Chinese men, on the other hand, were gen-

erally less that enthusiastic about traditional fashions until October 21, 2001. On that night, 20 APEC state leaders, including USA's George W. Bush and Russia's Vladimir Putin, appeared in Shanghai wearing traditional Chinese silk jackets. This caused an immediate sensation and sparked off not just a wave but a regular tsunami of male interest in traditional wear.

Just in case you didn't know, these traditional jackets are known as *tangzhuang* because their origins can be traced to the Tang Dynasty — China's golden age. This is why anything in anyway connected to that era has for many centuries been considered "very Chinese."

Fashion styles aside, all these clothes are made of the same material — silk. The Chinese have achieved almost impossible perfection in silk manufacture. Contemporary technique gives the fabric different looks and textures, making it appear and feel like linen, wool or cotton depending on the fabric's composition.

Well, I appear to be getting carried away by this topic, which is not surprising as the delightful sensation of fine silk on my skin reaffirms my pleasure in wearing it. In my view not only diamonds are a girl's only best friends, as silk from Hangzhou and Suzhou is of equal worth.

Handle with Care

The Chinese people are justly proud of their food, martial arts and traditional medicine, regarding them as China's national treasure. Millions overseas enjoy Chinese martial arts for physical fitness as well as self-defense. But as far as traditional Chinese medicine (TCM) is concerned, many have heard of it, but few put it to the test.

The *Huangdi Internal Canon* written in the 2nd century BC is to the Chinese what Hippocrates and his theories are for Europeans. It is the first written account of what is now known as traditional Chinese medicine. It coins the contemporary observation that it is better to stay healthy

Huangdi Internal Canon.

than fall ill in the words: "A wise man cures a disease before it becomes apparent and puts his organs in order before they fall into disrepair. Taking medicine after illness strikes and attempting to regulate health when it is in an abnormal state is like digging a well when thirsty or making weapons when a battle has already begun."

The achievements of ancient Chinese scientists are undeniably impressive. The principles of blood circulation were first

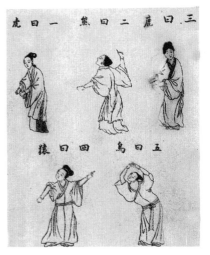

Hua Tuo paid great attention to prevention of diseases. He created a physical exercise imitating movements of five animals for people to keep fit.

ascribed to 16th and 17th century Europeans, but to second century BC Chinese physicians, circulation was as fundamental as the movement of the vital energy *qi*. As to the concept of bio-rhythms that didn't emerge in the West till 1960s, in ancient China the humblest of doctors knew the significance of a patient's "inner clock" when making diagnoses and prescribing treatments, also that asthma attacks are most serious at night when corticoid hormone secretion is lowest. The Chinese may also claim to be pioneers of endocrinology, as it was in the second century BC that they began to extract steroids from urine

Hua Tuo (c. 141-208), a renowned ancient Chinese physician.

for treatment of diseases, a process that was not discovered in Europe until 2,200 years later. Yet more proof of ancient Chinese medical prowess can be found in seventh century medical books, and the first description of the symptoms of diabetes. It was in 10th century China, as compared to 18th century Europe, that smallpox vaccination was put into practice.

Chinese and Western medicine work on entirely different principles. As a medical student friend once told me: "The only way to understand TCM is to disregard any Western medicine." Ancient Chinese medics paid scant attention to anatomy and had immense reservation about surgical operations. This stemmed from a different approach to healing. They regarded the human body as a mass of energy rather than a physical object, and believed health and longevity to be the products of daily renovation.

Chinese are above all convinced that good health depends upon the balance and harmony of each organ's *yin* and *yang*, and that their imbalance brings disease. Balance may be relative but imbalance is absolute, which is why humans are generally in a state of in-between. Chinese medicine works on holistic principles rather than treating discrete organs or areas, and is prescribed in order to maintain *yin/yang* equilibrium.

Working on these principles, Chinese doctors can more successfully treat certain diseases than European physicians, in particular kidney ailments and central nervous system disorders. A major advantage of TCM is that the herbal medicine it prescribes has few side effects.

European and American experts say that the main reason TCM has yet to achieve official recognition overseas is that there are no records of scientific experimentation to corroborate its effectiveness. To this charge, Chinese doctors say: "Yes, we have never conducted experiments on mice or other animals, but during our 4,000 years of practicing

A bronze model for acupunctuce.

TCM millions of people have been cured and had the quality of their lives improved. This seems to us ample experimental data." Such logical proof of the reliability and efficiency of TCM is impossible to refute.

Chinese practitioners of TCM believe that diseases and disorders are caused by six pathogenic factors, one of which, wind, is present in other five: cold, heat, dampness and summer sultriness. The negative impact of wind is apparent in chills that damage the vital energy qi, as coldness causes muscular spasms and upsets qi circulation. Dampness is at the root of headaches and dizziness, and dryness exhausts bodily fluids and is particularly bad for the lungs.

According to TCM doctors, the key factor to keeping and maintaining health is good spirits. Excessive emotions, desires and passions — both negative and positive — harm the health. Tradition prescribes avoidance of the seven emo-

Traditional medicine market in Kunming (Yunnan Province).

tions of joy, fear, depression, anxiety, sorrow, anger and fright. Depression and anger are bad for the liver, and anxiety and sorrow do harm to the spleen.

Good eating habits are regarded as main source of *qi*, and in these terms people nowadays eat excessively and their diet is unbalanced. The Chinese also believe that illness is the result of working too hard, taking insufficient rest and doing no exercise. To them, living this way is like spending more than you earn rather than putting a little away for a rainy day.

Different methods of medical treatment have developed in China over millennia. Rural physicians have always paid great attention to the healing power of plants, minerals and substances of animal origin. Chinese pharmacology probably encompasses the world's most comprehensive range of drugs. Looking inside an average medicine store, dried snakes, seahorses, scorpions and powdered antler immediately spring to view, as well as prosaic pills, powders and tablets.

Chinese herbal medicines.

Another approach is one of influencing organism's vital points, better known as acupuncture. This was first mentioned in medical books of the Han Dynasty (206 BC-AD 220) and has long since been perfected. There are 12 types of needle manipulation that work on the principle of stimulating or suppressing the function of a specific organ.

There is no modern scientific explanation why acupuncture is so effective, only the TCM principle that needles applied to specific points correspond to certain organs and connect the energy meridians through which *qi* moves. A needle can block the stream of meridian energy, but exactly how is unclear.

Traditional Chinese medicine still has many unexplained areas. It is said that TCM can work miracles, but in these rational times not miracles but detailed explanations are required. This is a tall order for TCM, as in many cases Chinese practitioners themselves cannot give precise analyses of how or why their treatment and remedies work.

But then, is it really that important for a sick person to know how he or she recovers from an ailment? To my mind, most important is that traditional Chinese medicine has healed people for centuries. Isn't this the main aim of medical doctors the world over?

2

The Main Value

What Is in a Name?

The first surname surprise struck me when I was a schoolgirl. In another class of my school there was a student bearing the same family name as mine — Katsubo. I considered myself unlucky with so many classmates not having their namesakes. Then I got married and adopted my husband's name thus becoming Pleskacheuskaya. This is a usual confusion with female surnames in my country. I have two female cousins born with the same family name as mine — Katsubo — but these days they are Tarabenko and Yushkovskaya and it is hardly believable three of us have the same grandmother. Very often I think that Chinese in this regard are wiser than we are: females generally don't adopt their husbands' names when getting married. Very likely they are right: what is given at birth determines fate.

What is more important — individual or society? Rhetorical question, one that could be argued for life time. To my mind, in many aspects family names mirror the national values. For example, in China if a person's name is Zhang Wei, then Zhang is a surname. In other words the Chinese determines his affiliation with the family clan and then his place in this clan — in our case name Wei. Friends and colleagues address each other by surname, not a name. In case if Zhang is an elderly person he can be referred to as "Lao Zhang" (old Zhang) and if he is a teenager people would call him "Xiao Zhang" (young Zhang). This rule is firm and obeyed.

Nowadays China (at least its big cities) is strongly affected by Westernization. Rules of naming are undergoing changes even if not quickly. Many Chinese communicating with foreigners on a daily basis adopt foreign names — just for convenience. But you also have to be prepared to adopt a Chinese name if entering the Heavenly Kingdom for a long period of time. This adopted Chinese name would be written in all official papers.

If the name of your fellow Chinese friend is among *laobaixing* ("one hundred old family names"), it means he is inseparable part of the state he lives in. But in the country with 1.3 billion people is it enough to have just 100 surnames? Thus the one of the most amazing problems China faces today is a shortage of family names.

Scientists and officials advise people to be more resourceful naming their children; it will help in future to avoid confusion. Some Chinese have names and surnames of two characters each. But such

lucky people are more exception than a rule. Most Chinese have surname written with the only character and name written with one or two. This problem is especially topical for big cities in which thousands of people have the same names written with the same characters. Chinese newspapers quite often publish stories on erroneous arrests, bank accounts

Clay figurines made in Wuxi, Jiangsu Province.

mistakes or even fallacious surgeries — all these because of name confusion.

Recent survey discovered that nowadays there are around 3,100 family names in use in China, but 99.4 percent of the population are squeezed in just 500 of them. Just imagine — quarter of the country's population, near 350 million, share just five surnames — Li, Wang, Zhang, Liu and Chen. In Beijing alone there are more than 5,000 people named Zhang Li and Liu Hui. There is no surprise at all that boundaries of many parts of the country remain virtually the same for almost 4,000 years and the local people are proud of their close relations with the ancestors bearing the same family name. The seven most widespread Chinese surnames are Li, Wang, Zhang, Liu, Chen, Yang and Zhao and they were used as early as the Song Dynasty (960-1278). Authors of the fundamental scientific research *One Hundred Modern Chinese Surnames* maintain that during the whole Chinese history some 10,000 family names have been in use.

The fact that 100 million of the Chinese can be described as the "average Zhao" on the one hand makes easier generalizations and work of sociologists. But how difficult it was for indigenous population in times when the country was ruled by the foreigners! During the Mongolian Yuan Dynasty (1271-1368) one of the provincial rulers named Zaixiang Boyan (see the difference?) was so set against dominating Han popula-

tion that in 1337 he appealed to the Emperor Shun
for permission to kill every resident of his province
surnamed Zhang, Wang, Liu, Li and Zhao. The action might have been simple and effective way to
finish off huge number of people. Luckily, the emperor refused this appeal.

Tongli, Jiangsu Province.

Power and prestige played a big role in surviv-
ing or, on the contrary, in eradicating family names
in history. Surname Zhao experienced its heyday
during the Song Dynasty, Liu was in zenith during
the Han Dynasty (206 BC-AD 220) and Li became
the most spread during the Tang Dynasty (618-907).

Family name Wang literally means prince or
ruler and the majority of ancestors of the modern
bearer of this name probably had royal blood. The

A Man on a Horse, by Yuan-dynasty artist Zhao Mengfu (1254-1322). There are many seals on the painting, some of which contain the name of the artist.

most famous story about the origins of this name tells about inventive heir to the throne lived during the Eastern Zhou Dynasty. When the boy was 15 years old, he dared to advise his father, the emperor, on how to cope with flood. For this impudence he was deprived of the right to ascend the throne. With time descendants of the young prodigy dissolved amongst commoners but kept calling their clan Wang in memory of the might-have-been emperor.

The story of Li family name that translated as plum is not that simple. It can be traced as far back as to the court of the legendary ruler Huangdi, the Yellow Emperor. His principle adviser was a person named Mu Tao. He had the title Da Li, or the head of the emperor's court. It is claimed that a magic unicorn with abilities to tell the difference between truth and lies was his helper. Moreover, this unicorn used his horn to kill infringers. Because Mu Tao was strong and fair, later during Xia and Shang (1600-1046 BC) periods the name Li became associated with order, principle and justice and was rather popular.

Ironically, the character for this surname has been changed in 11th century BC, when Emperor Zhou of the Shang Dynasty executed his head judge Li Zheng. His wife and a child escaping from death made their way to the remote kingdom and nearly starved to death during the trip. They survived on eating plums growing on trees along the road. So, 90 million contemporary Lis in some way give due to this event. But of course not all of them-some of them are likely the descendants of the Taoism founder Lao Zi, as he was also surnamed Li.

Well, talking about sages, don't forget the greatest of them (at least as people in China think) — Confucius. I have a feeling that people in his home town Qufu and outskirts properly share his name Kong. It can also be met around Shaoxing City to which some of the Great Teacher's descendants moved centuries ago. Group of my colleagues from Belarus once visited Qufu and told me after the visit about dining experience with one of the Confucius descendants. This is true — they are still living in the home town of the great sage. Generally, almost all family names that are in use today in China originate from some outstanding historical figures.

Some Chinese names, especially those not widespread, basically concentrated in one or two

localities often originate from the rulers of an ancient state or identify themselves with a definite ethnos living in the region. The surname Tan, that is widespread in Hubei Province today, was first mentioned during the Han Dynasty when the local population regarded as a barbarian a person named Tan Zhun. Since that time this family name was often given to minorities' representatives.

Well then, who is number one in China? Recently statistics affirmed that the first position is taken by Wangs — there are around 100 million of them in mainland China. But population census of 2000 changed the picture in favor of Zhangs: there are more than 0.1 billion of people with such name. So, it is very likely Zhang is the most widespread family name in the world. Lis finished third in this race.

Wedding of Yesterday and Today

During previous hundreds of years wedding ceremonies in China changed dramatically and, taking into account China's turbulent history, it does not come as a surprise.

Ancient wedding ceremony consisted of six rituals: gifts-giving, auspicious blessings during engagement, welcoming of the newlyweds, etc. Usually the parents of a boy reaching marrying age would invite a matchmaker. The matchmaker possessed many tablets — similar to nowadays' name cards — with names and ages of brides-to-be on them. Then the matchmaker would approach an eligible girl's parents and give an introduction to them about the groom-to-be. If the two sides agreed, a meeting would be arranged. A woman holding the highest position in the boy's family chose an auspicious date for the first encounter with the girl's family. The main purpose of such meeting was to appreciate the future daughter-in-law's appearance and character as well as financial position of her family. It was strictly prohibited for the girl to see her husband before the marriage.

Betrothal and engagement were the main ceremonies. According to popular traditions, the engagement was more important than any laws, it was next to impossible to change anything after the couple was engaged. Cancellation of the engagement was an ultimate disgrace to the family.

One of the most magnificent parts of the wedding ceremony is welcoming of the bride. She was dressed up in red as it is the color of happiness and prosperity. After the bride took her seat in a wedding sedan-chair, the wedding ceremony started. During the whole ceremony, the bride's face was covered with a red scarf with an image of a dragon on it to drive away evil spirits. The bride was expected to cry during all her way to the groom' house, it was demonstration of her love and attachment to the parental home.

The main part of the ceremony started when the bride arrived at the groom's house. In some regions she had to step over a basin with fire purposefully placed in front of the house. It was a sign that everything bad and evil is burnt. In other regions the bride had to step over a saddle holding a vase in her hands. In Chinese language the last characters of the words for "vase" and "saddle" taking together mean peace and prosperity.

Then the newlyweds stepped into the sitting-room and kowtowed to Heaven and Earth, parents and — at last — to each other. Then they exchanged bowls filled with wine (in some regions they mixed wines from their respective bowls and then poured this "joint" wine) and drank it. Then they cut a little bit of each other's hair for keeping them as a symbol of unity. The wedding banquet was a culmination of the ceremony as the bride went around the guests offering wine and various foods.

The final ritual took place in the newlyweds' room. They sat down on a bed on which peanuts, dates, nuts and *longan* fruit have been purposefully scattered. Meaning of the characters representing these presents was "to give birth to a son as soon as possible." It was the first time the groom saw the face of his now wife by taking away the red scarf covering her face.

One of the first laws adopted by New China was the Marriage Law which came into force on May 1, 1950, just 6 months after establishing of the People's Republic of China. In a sense it was a breakthrough for the country declaring for the first time in its history gender equality,

monogamy and right for divorce.

Today traditional wedding ceremony in most cases is merely for tourists' attraction.

Everything was in red color for weddings in the 1950s. The country is really lucky that old auspicious and new revolutionary colors are the same. Thus brides could easily get dressed in red as it was in vogue again. Rural brides wore traditional red dresses but young urbanites being more sensitive to fashion dressed themselves up in suits a la Mao Zedong. Wedding dresses (in villages) and suits (in cities) were supplemented by big red paper flowers. The principal guest of the weddings might be the Secretary of the Party Committee of a factory at which one of the newlyweds worked. Marriage certificate with inscriptions like "Freedom of

Today traditional wedding ceremony in most cases is merely for tourists' attraction.

Marriage," "Equality of Women and Men" was signed by bride, groom, matchmaker, witness and parents of bride and groom. Then a banquet was held. Every guest usually presented a couple 5 *jiao* (0.5 yuan) and other practical gifts such as pans, mirrors, jugs, wash-stand, etc.

In many cases urban intelligentsia and Party cadres canceled a wedding banquet and the most fashionable gift in those circles was the book *How the Steel Is Tempered* by the Soviet revolutionary-turned writer Nikolai Ostrovskiy.

Weddings during the "cultural revolution" were strongly

politicized, painted in revolutionary red with extremely simple ceremony.

In 1967 Zhong Miaoshen decided to get married on the 1st of May as it was usual to choose wedding days to coincide with the festivals. In local register office newlyweds got the marriage certificate with inscription: "Our principal leadership is the Communist Party of China and the theoretical base of our ideology is Marxism and Leninism." There was no unified form of marriage certificates and every region had something special written in the document.

Zhong Miaoshen and his wife received ten copies of the "Three Selected Works by Mao Zedong" and around 6 plaster statuettes of the leader as their wedding gifts. Walls of their wedding room had been decorated with portraits of Mao and the red character for loyalty. Colleagues presented framed words: "To read books of Chairman Mao, listen to his words and be his good soldiers." There was just one thing with no relation to politics — character "double happiness" which was used in China from of old as decoration for the newlyweds' room.

Such lively papercut can often be found on window panes on the occasion of wedding.

During the 1970s weddings became even more unpretentious as grain and other foodstuffs as well as cigarettes were distributed by coupons. There were no special food coupons for weddings and for holding a banquet, families of bride and groom had to cut down their usual food allowance. After getting the marriage certificate, newlyweds got coupons for obtaining a buffet, a bed and chairs.

By the way, in my home country, former Soviet Union, newlyweds-to-be got special coupons until as late as the beginning of 1990s. I got married in 1988 and after submission of application to the local registry office we got coupons for a visit to the special shop selling wedding dresses and suits, shoes and vodka.

At the beginning of the 1980s, new Chinese policy of the reforms and opening-up altered wedding ceremonies. On April 9, 1989, Li Jing celebrated her birthday and appointed the wedding ceremony on this day too. That time permanent wave was in vogue, and Li Jing spent half of a day doing it. She and her groom spent literally hours in photo studio making colored pictures, real family treasure as all pictures before were mere black and white.

The wedding banquet was held in a restaurant and it was real luxury during those times when a dinner in a restaurant was regarded as a special event ventured by people with good *guanxi* (connections). Practicality was fashionable again and presents were well matched with this trend: photo frames, tea sets, woolen blankets and quartz clocks. The newlyweds have even been granted 15-days vacation for honey-moon-luxury their parents couldn't even dream of!

It was how the new epoch bringing Westernized weddings started — down with traditional red dress and linen shoes, long live white veil and tie!

Traditional wedding ceremony.

New epoch brought new prices — it is impossible to hold a banquet with 50 yuan and to get off with 5 *jiao* as a wedding present these days. Traditional set of wedding photos costs no less than 2,400 yuan. Wedding ceremonies nowadays is a big and profitable industry with professional staff, special web sites, magazines, cars, masters of ceremonies and companies arranging "unforgettable honey-moon."

Urban newlyweds spend around 8,200-24,800 yuan to hold an "adequate" wedding that often serves as a symbol of prosperity and social status. In China demonstration of material well-being is closely connected to conceptions of "face" and prestige which are very important ideas.

Grandiose weddings have renewed ancient tradition of red envelops. They are used for money-gift; the amount should be divisible by 40 and giving much means showing prosperity. Thus most of expenses for the wedding banquets usually are repaid.

After a number of years priorities in choosing an "ideal husband" have been changed drastically.

During the 1950s, women preferred to marry workers for their stable income; during the 1960s, marriages with peasants were in vogue, those men were valued for their unproblematic economical and political status. Military personnel were popular choice for getting married during the 1970s because of their secure job and material well-being. During the 1980s, after the reforms and opening-up started the most successful marriage was that with diplomat or intellectual. The practical 1990s sorted things out and a groom's occupation was not that important. Nowadays modern girls are attracted by money, own apartment and a car.

However, many old traditions are very much alive these days. Departure of a bride is still the most vivid event during the wedding ceremony. Red sedan chair is replaced by four cars with the first one decorated by flowers and characters "double happiness." The groom is usually accompanied by a witness (or rather several of them), uncles and two witnesses to the

Grasslands, clear blue skies and white yurts can be seen in most part of the Inner Mongolia Autonomous Region.

bride. Before this delegation enters the bride's home, a big noise is arranged — in cities people pierce balloons and in villages as custom people blow firecrackers. This is a signal

for the bride: be ready. The bride's witnesses ask the groom various questions: for example, what is the favorite color of his sweetheart and others — for making sure that the couple know each other well. After the groom enters the house he presents her with a bouquet of flowers and makes a photo with all her extended family. Then a procession leaves the house for the wedding banquet. Usually parents of the bride do not attend the banquet as for ages they were expected to grieve losing a daughter. Nowadays many urban brides demand their parents' presence during the banquet but village girls don't dream such a thing yet. When the bride approaches the car the groom takes off her shoes and changed them for a new red pair. Red is for happiness and new as a symbol of new life. Changing shoes is an old ritual meaning that the bride should not bring earth from her parental house into her new home on soles of her shoes as her previous life should be left behind. Then the procession leaves. Route for the cars is planned thoroughly as tradition demands it being in a shape of a circle as it is a symbol of eternal marriage. Sometimes the bride brings a rooster with a hen waiting for him in the newlyweds' bedroom. It means that children will appear in this marriage as soon as the hen lays an egg.

The wedding ceremony itself lasts for merely 20 minutes as a master of ceremonies reads the marriage certificate and tells how the couple met for the first time. Usually this ceremony is lively and cheerful accompanied with jokes and laughs. Often the bride receives an envelope with 1,001 yuan in it symbolizing that she was chosen out of thousands. The couple bows to parents of the groom as a sign of respect and obeisance. Guests arrive at the dinner-time and newlyweds and their parents walk around all tables and toast for happiness of the new family.

One Family, One Child

For both my native Belarus and China question of population increase is a headache, but of different nature: in my country the authorities try all possible means to convince women to give more births to increase Belarus population. On the contrary, the Chinese authorities dream about population decrease and work hard to achieve this aim. According to population forecast, it is expected that population will peak at 1.6 billion — and it is only for mainland China, without Hong Kong, Macao and Taiwan.

In 1949 when the People's Republic of China was established, population of the country was around 542 million and 20 years later it increased by enormous 265 million. It was that time the government faced the challenge: if birth rate remained the same, taking into account the economic situation of that time, the country might have been confronted with threat of starvation. This was the main reason behind the new family planning policy adopted in the 1970s.

At the very beginning of 2005, population of mainland China reached 1.3 billion. According to population forecast, in 2010 there will be 1.4 billion Chinese on the mainland. The state strongly advises to the citizens not to go beyond one child per family. However, it is not entirely correct to refer to this policy as to "one family, one child." For example, in rural areas several years after giving birth to the first child the second attempt is allowed — in case if the first child is a girl. This is birth control with Chinese specifics caused by the farmers' preference towards boys. The authorities conduct an explanatory campaign convincing people that gender doesn't matter and boys and girls are of equal value for the family. For a newcomer to China it may seem strange but actually this trend reflects ancient traditions and culture of the country. Nowadays pension system is on the stage of formation. Traditions and laws demand children to support their elderly parents. Good boys were traditionally regarded as hard working, raising more money, more enduring and — last but not least — not wasting their time on giving birth. This is conservative way of thinking. Meanwhile, active campaign with a slogan "Girls are not inferior to boys!" yields fruits, and gender imbalance, which is regarded as a potential threat to the stable society, is gradually decreasing.

A Uygur boy in Xinjiang

Majority of restrictions apply to people of mainly the Han ethnic group which constitutes 92 percent of China's population. There are 55 other ethnic minorities living in the country — Zhuang, Manchu, Hui, Miao, Uygur and others. Among those others are even Russians, officially only 13,500 of them living in

China. Quantity of some minorities could easily constitute population of a middle-sized European country: there are 5 million Mongols, around 4.6 million Tibetans and 15.5 million Zhuangs living in China. They are allowed to have 2-3 children in a family. For the smallest minorities such as Lhoba (2,300 people), Gaoshan (2,900), Hezhen (4,300), there are no restrictions at all — it is up to them to decide how many children they want.

Birth rate is around 1.07 percent today. It does not sound as a big figure but it means 12.79 million people every year — more than the population of my native Belarus or, for example, Hungary. Moreover, it

means that every year quarter of increased national income is spent on newborns.

China's official family policy is late marriages, late childbirth. There are around 352 million women of childbearing age in China and 251 million of them are married. There are virtually no unwed-mothers in classical sense and should not be — it is next to impossible for an unmarried woman to get permission for giving birth. In most cases abortion is the only way out for an unexpectedly pregnant woman. In China abortion is also the most widespread family planning tool practicing by 45.5 percent of women. The second position in this regard is taken by female sterilization — 38.2 percent. Surprising fact is that half of all world men gone under knife to make vasectomy (male sterilization) are Chinese — there are around 20 million of them.

Children enjoying a game.

Every year the authorities spend around 36 million USD distributing condoms for free, more than 200 million married couples regularly use them. The official state family planning policy is backed up by overwhelming majority of Chinese people.

Every year around 200,000 babies are born unhealthy and many of them remain disabled for the whole of their lives. Unhealthy children and invalids are distress and a hard burden for any family. For Chinese parents it might have been a tragedy if the state didn't foresee this nuance in family planning policy. If a child is disabled and it is obvious he/she would be unable in future to support himself/herself, the family would get permission to give another birth.

The family planning policy has been in practice for more than 30 years now, meaning that at least one generation grew up as the only child in a family. Now they get married and think about having children. The authorities have made the decision aimed at these young people. If both husband and wife are the only children in their respective families they are allowed to have two children. Of course if they want to, the only term is that four years at least should elapse between birth of the first and the second child.

Another unexpected trend has become evident these years that many well-to-do women with high income are not willing to have a child, let alone two. For example, around 10 percent of families living in China's capital city Beijing prefer not having children. In three richest cities of the mainland — Beijing, Shanghai and Guangzhou — there are around 600,000 such couples in total.

Many women explain their reluctance to have children: "If I do not have children, I am always a child myself." So, recently a new law was adopted guaranteeing males and females equal rights in childbirth. It does not mean of course that men are allowed to give birth — in this case Mother Nature would have its strong protest. It stipulates that a married woman must consult her husband if she has got pregnant and is willing to make abortion.

Miao people are eligible to have two children.

You may see now that birth control is a tough thing in every country practicing it — despite that the authorities would like to increase it, as in Belarus, or to decrease it, as in China.

Deputies of the National People's Congress, the main legislative organ of the country.

The old conception *duozi-duofu* (more children-more happiness) for a time led to uncontrollable expansion of population in China, which, correspondingly, affected quality of people. Timely adoption of family planning, promotion of the conception of "less children, better quality" not only brought fast population growth to a halt, but also enhanced quality of people. However, the Chinese people all hope that their children would one day become "dragons" and realize their best values. The "object-choosing game" described below has reflected such conception and is still in practice today.

In the old days, Chinese children faced the first test on their first birthday. This semiserious game had been practiced in China since ancient times with an aim to determine a child's future. After the festive dinner marking the baby's first year, parents put in front of the child numerous objects in order to determine his/her inclinations. Scientists are sure that this game was already in vogue during the Northern and Southern Dynasties (386-589). Among the objects to choose from were books, toys, cosmetics, jewelry, flowers, money and other things brought in by guests and relatives. The child was placed in front of these objects, all with symbolic meaning. Parents held their breath waiting for the child making a choice — what he/she would grasp. Many people thought that the best choice was a book. If it was the book the child grasped first, it meant he/she would become passionate reader, and if gods were in good mood, it was very likely the baby would grow into fame as a scholar. Book choice was a pride to every parent.

The most desired professions for Chinese children are military or police man, teacher, doctor and scientist. Among the people admired by Chinese children are heroes, stars of show business and sport and scientists.

Demands Chinese parents have of their children are, among others, modesty, respecting the elderly, enterprising, bringing honor to the family. Future success of a child is not something entirely personal, but closely connected with longings of several generations of a family. At present, particularly in cities like Beijing and Shanghai, parents' input, both in terms of money and time, in raising a child is huge. They spend almost all their spare time on their child, urging him/her to study diligently, to do physical exercises to keep fit, etc.

To raise children in today's China is not cheap, in big cities in particular. "Calculate," suggested 28-year-old Liu.

Long and expensive journey starts long before a baby is born. During nine months of pregnancy expenses of mother-to-be average around 5,000 yuan — for regular medical

Spring outing.

check-ups, analysis, food and clothes. In some cases expenses could be as high as 20,000 yuan.

"My son is not even one year old but he already costs us dear," Liu continued. Every month the family spends around 1,500 yuan on food, nursing and medical care. Xie Qing, 35 in age, manager of an export company in Beijing, agreed by saying, "My six-year-old son doesn't yet know what money is but his life is tightly connected to it." Like many other contemporary Chinese parents, Xie sent her son to a well-reputed kindergarten to be raised in "proper" atmosphere. Such atmosphere however doesn't come cheap and costs around 15,000 yuan a year.

Many parents are sure that the only child in a family should be raised harmoniously. Xu Baoyu, forty-year-old employee of a Beijing scientific research institute, accompanies Fu Lin, her seven-year-old daughter, to a musical school every Saturday. Piano lessons cost around 500 yuan a month that is quite a burden for the middle class family, but Xu is sure that the only child should get the best of everything.

However, blind deep love for a child, when going to the extreme, might result in a child's waywardness or being spoilt, hence the term "little emperor." In the feudal days, an emperor was a supreme ruler and all people must obey his rule. If a kid has behaved like a "little emperor," and his/her parents do whatever their child requests, such a "little emperor" is most likely selfish, which runs counter to the Chinese tradition of being modest and tolerant. Many parents have realized this and given more attention to developing the character of a child in a comprehensive way.

Problem of the only child being egoist is the topical one for China. A recent research conducted by scientists has brought to light how the only children in families are raised — in fact, it is

Town of Wuxi in Jiangsu Province is famous for its clay painted figurines.

easy for them to communicate with others and make friends. Don't forget that by nature the Chinese (like Russians or Italians for example) are collectivists, they prefer to bring their joys, achievements and even problems into community. Nowadays traditional way of life in cities is changing and it is very likely that after next generation it will change forever but today it is mostly like it used to be some 100-200 years ago. What are criterions for the little Chinese to make friends? "Activity and good school marks" comes first, then "bright personality and good abilities" and "ability for good communication." Scientists undertaking this research affirm that the only child in a family develops faster, is full of energy and has various interests.

A Hundred Family Lock worn by a baby after a certain period of time. Made of silver donated by many families, it was said to be able to keep the baby fit and strong.

The ancient Chinese treated their children in different manner. For example, they counted one's age from conception and every New Year added one year of life. Before getting three years old, a child was not even considered a person and in case of death didn't get funeral. Maturing automatically raised a person's social status.

During first two to three years, a child was taken as his/her parents' continuation: sleeping and eating with them, a baby was tied to the mother's back and traveled around this way. Mother fed an infant every time he/she started to cry and breast — feeding continued for a long period of time — usually until a baby reached age of three to four years and in some cases even longer.

Who Wants to Be a God?

Amongst my most amazing impressions of China are those of elderly people. Wake up early, around six in the morning, and go out to the streets — you will watch big groups of elders doing exercises and dancing with fans. There are nearly no youngsters in such groups as they have many good reasons to ignore morning activities — sleeping late, going to work and simply having more important things to do. But grandpas and grandmas self-lessly make strokes with swords, jolt fans to the accompaniment of drum and cymbals and obviously enjoy themselves. This pleasure and enjoyment is not limited only to the morning collective exercises but lasts all day long, peaking again during evening dancing. Warm Beijing evening is filled with hissing sounds of old cassette recorders or with familiar sounds of drums and cymbals — it is time to dance. The same elderly people in pairs or one by one move enthusiastically.

Many elder Chinese are sure that winter swimming is beneficial for health. Harbin (Heilongjiang Province).

Such calligraphy practice is very popular with old Chinese men.

Take another morning entertainment — calligraphy. In China characters inscription has always been considered an art, calligraphic poems are exhibited in museums and galleries along with pictures. Good calligrapher has a strong hand and thus writing characters is a kind of physical exercise. Every Beijing park is full of elderly people (one small detail — there is nearly no women among them) writing poems on a pavement or stone plates with a long stick with a sponge at its end used instead of a brush. Sponge is often moistened with water. These calligraphic masterpieces are quick to dry but writers are not distressed — they start their exercises again and again.

The favorite daytime entertainment of the

In the morning people are dancing in parks all over the country.

aged is chess. In China this game is not an individual sport as we used to think but a collective one. Near houses and along cities' highways, big groups of old men gather, divide into teams and — go ahead, the game starts! One moves figures and the team actively and noisily elaborates strategy and tactics.

God of Longevity.

Simple pleasures like drinking tea and talking about bygone youth are also very popular. Elders seat together, drink their tea, talking slowly but one of them suddenly suggests something like "why not do some *taiji*?," others nod assent, stand up, make some stances and move and then go back to their routine — tea and talking. It is a touching picture, indeed.

Attitude of the Chinese to the aged is very different from that we have back home. According to local ideas, at the age of 60, a brand new life starts. This idea comes from zodiac beliefs. Previous astrological cycle — five times by 12 years, full turnover of the astrological circle — is finished and it is time to get all possible pleasures of life.

Filial piety is the fundamental principle of China's traditional way of life, unshakable for centuries. If unchallenged and never doubted respect towards elders, parents and superiors were gone, then China will lose its roots. And a tree without roots can not survive.

Filial piety and respect is fundament of all fundaments, the most important of all Confucius maxims. Filial piety and concern about elders are source of all virtues. China has many stories about model examples of filial piety telling about loving sons and daughters. One of the most striking examples of such piety is Emperor Qianlong himself (r. 1736-1796) under whom China was considered the most

Elder Chinese like to chat with each other. The scene in this photo can be seen at every street corner, especially in summertime. People sit together, chatting and discussing things of their younger years and plans for future.

prosperous country of the world. Qianlong voluntarily retired from the state affairs after 60 years on the throne — just because his grandfather Emperor Kangxi ruled for the same number of years. Qianlong didn't want somebody to doubt his respect for his grandfather — who was great emperor — by ruling longer than he had done.

An old Uygur (Xinjiang Uygur Autonomous Region).

Existed family rituals verify clan hierarchy and some of those rituals living up to these days have modified a little. Family members gathering around the table during lunar New Year celebrations used to kowtow to the family patriarch saying "I owe!" A saying goes: "If you do not obey to elders you will live 10 years less."

There was proper upbringing in China. Customs did not allow not only disrespect for elders but also condemnation of any aggressive behavior of children because family in China has always been

considered a prototype of the society: anything threatening to peace and harmony of the family potentially can destroy stability of the society.

Policy was a continuation of the family way of life. Attitude towards the head of the family was repeated in attitude towards a superior and further along all bureaucratic hierarchy right up to the emperor. In some aspects these relationships are still in place that make easier building socialism with Chinese specifics and implementing reforms. Confucius' canons affirm that for good ruling of the country the ruler must cope with family affairs and troubles very well and for maintaining peace in the family one must devote him to self-education.

Without question, many things changed but filial piety is one of the corner stones on which China has been built. This is one of the reasons for such a moving attitude towards the aged. For every 100,000 people in the country there are three of 100 years old and older on average. In some regions the number is higher which is surge of pride for both local authorities and inhabitants of the blessed region. For example, there are 122 centenarians in the city of Leshan, Sichuan Province. Researchers think that the main reasons for such long-living are geographical position and environment. Scientists also believe that other factors such as physical labor, open character, material sufficiency and filial children are of equal importance. Those living a long life usually enjoy harmonious family relations and often themselves are model examples of filial piety. They are respected members of the family and enjoy the life that has turned out exactly as the ancient Chinese rule promised: when you grow old you are the respected and well-to-do person enjoying simple pleasures of life.

Many retired Chinese start to do things they were dreaming about all their lives: for example, painting.

Another famous place for the aged in China is Hainan Island. It is often referred to as "Longevity Island" as there are more than 90,000 people older than 90. In 2001 the local authorities held a special festival to choose the island's "God of Longevity."

When the competition was announced nearly all 90-year-old local people presented their applications willing to become gods. One 96-year-old man went 2.5 kilometers to submit his application in person. Asked why he didn't send grandson or great-grandson, he answered proudly: "Are there any other possibilities to prove I am healthy?" The point is that the competition terms were strict: competitors should be at least 90 years old, in good health, with strong legs and hands, good vision and hearing, they should be able to make some work in fields, communicate with others on a regular basis, to have a good family and good relations with neighbors and — last but not least — to be enthusiastic for healthy life style. Not every young man can comply with all these requirements, let alone grandpas and grandmas!

Thirty-nine elders made it to the final and every one of them was awarded with the title "Outstanding Hainan Old Resident." Hu Kaiyuan, 110 years old, was declared the "God of Longevity" for his good health, harmonious family relations and venerable age. While awarding the certificate Hainan Vice-Governor wished Hu Kaiyuan to live up to 200 years. "Thank you," answered the old man, "but my son wished me to live up to 300 years." Everybody in attendance laughed quite long after these words.

What are the secrets of long-living? Elders of Hainan say they are work and good mood. Take "God" Hu for an example: all his life he worked in the field and went fishing at sea. Even after he celebrated

centenary he is able to go one kilometer to his son's shop to chat with friends.

Good talk to friends is the favourite pastime of many elder Chinese females.

What do you think about traditional Chinese family? Three or four generations living under one roof: bald-headed and white-bearded great-great-grandfather living together with five grandpas, ten fathers and dozens of children. It is next to impossible to find such a family in contemporary China. That was the ancient custom — surrounded by grandchildren and great-grandchildren, the old saw

"Veselyi Veter" choir in Beijing. Many of its participants worked with specialists from the Soviet Union or studied in the Soviet Union in the 1950s.

that their life was not for nothing. Children, for their turn, know that when they grow old they also would have peaceful and easy old years and if they fall sick there always be somebody to take care of them. This was the Chinese way of life.

In recent years a new trend has come to life — parents and children live separately. Widowed elders try to marry again as the traditional conception of four musts for the old Chinese — house, savings, wife (husband) and friends — is still very much alive.

There are more than 132 million people in China at the age of 60 and older. It is expected there will be around 400 million of them in 2050, quarter of all the population of the country.

3

Everlasting Feast

Heavenly Pleasures

Many specialists think that world gastronomic variety can be divided into three main groups: French, Middle East and Chinese cuisines. There are people who do not agree: Italians will bombard you with pizza and pasta, Spaniards have paella, and even my fellow Belarusians can take part in this argument with our famous potato pancakes — *draniki*. Many Americans also think that pizza and pancakes belong to their national cuisine. Once I had a hot dispute on this matter with an American woman.

Bright colors of Kashgar bazaar (Xinjiang Uygur Autonomous Region).

I presented my strongest argument: "My ancestors had pancakes on their dining tables centuries before America has even been discovered!"

Despite all these arguments, one thing is for sure — the Chinese phenomenon deserves a very special place in the world's recipe books as well as in our hearts. Chinese people themselves consider their cuisine as the "brightest pearl" of their culture. And justly so.

Food for Chinese people is a genuine cult, exquisite art and a source of candid pleasure — all in one. Chinese people never "have a bite," they even don't have such a phrase in their vocabulary — they eat thoroughly and quickly. Traditional Chinese greeting words "*chi fan le ma*?" can be translated as "Did you eat?" Out of necessity, Chinese people have managed to eat nearly everything growing, moving or flying. This necessity has been turned into virtue and now Chinese cuisine boasts nearly 5,000 dishes catering to any taste. These dishes are divided into styles and varieties depending on geography, ethnic group or social status of their creators, adaptors and eaters — family and temple styles, official, palace or medicinal dishes. Foods are separated into hot, cold, formal, sweet dishes and soups, depending on the cooking style. Specificity of the Chinese cuisine means that no dish can be separated from its origin: Geography, climate, natu-

Ham and Beancurd.

ral resources, local traditions, social and cultural factors are all relevant.

Foods in Chinese cuisine traditionally belong to two categories: main and additional. Main or staple foods are carbohydrates; meat, fish and vegetables have always been considered additional. Chinese culinary arts comprise a combination of the two. Chinese chefs also use additional seasoning and condiments, especially for meat and fish dishes. For ages, five main seasonings that correspond to the five humors have distinguished Chinese food: ginger is pungent, vinegar is sour, salt is savory, wine is bitter and syrup is sweet. It was in the Middle Ages that the popular flavoring soy sauce came into use.

English-speaking people assert that foundation of Chinese cuisine consists of three G's: garlic, ginger and green onion. Probably this is an explanation for the famous pungency. But not all local dishes are spicy; there are many with a mild or subtle flavor. Additionally, Chinese people use little salt but sauces and seasonings instead.

Shrimps with Green Peppers.

Philosophy is present in every aspect of everyday life in China, and culinary art is no exception. The difference between main and additional foods demonstrates the principle of balance between *yin* and *yang*. Most fruits and vegetables belong to *yin*, they are moist and soft with a cooling effect and nourish the feminine aspect of our nature. *Yang* food is fried, hot, often

Food stalls near Wangfujing Street.

including red meat and warms, and nourishes the masculine part of us. As *yin* and *yang* compliment each other in philosophy, so they do in food. This is why Chinese people never add soy sauce to rice: they both belong to the *yang* group and eating them together causes imbalance.

Another philosophical principle used often in Chinese cuisine is "to place true into false." Within this concept, the aim of any Chinese chef is to obscure the ingredients of a dish. Consequently, Buddhist monks who are supposed to be vegetarians don't even notice that they are not eating meat as there are so many vegetarian dishes resembling meat and fish in form and taste, such as "roast meat" made of soy beans or "fish" made of eggs.

China is a vast country whose peoples enjoy different flavors. The most obvious difference is that rice is the staple food of southerners while northerners prefer noodles, steamed

buns, etc. Nearly every province and even some cities have their trademark dishes: Beijing has roast duck, Yangzhou has fried rice and Suzhou has shellfish. One of the most famous Guangdong dishes is "Dragon and Tiger Battle" made of three kinds of poisonous snake, wildcat and seasonings. It is extremely hard to find a restaurant with this dish on its menu as the SARS outbreak in 2003 prompted many restaurants to stop serving civet-cat.

Food in China is not just for filling the stomach; it is imbued with sig-nificance, especially on traditional lunar calendar holidays. Almost every dish on a table has meaning: oranges and chicken for good luck, fish for bounty and chestnuts and *tofu* for wealth. During marriage celebrations, newlyweds eat sweet balls made of glutinous rice

One of the most popular street snacks sold all over the country from autumn to spring is hawthorn coated in caramel on a stick — *bingtang hulu.*

to ensure a sweet and harmonious marriage. Parents and guests pour nuts, dates, candies and oranges on the marital bed in hopes of inspiring a son. When a baby is one month old, its mother would present boiled eggs dyed red to relatives, neighbors and friends, meaning that the mother is cleansed and can visit the temple to pray.

Mandarin Fish with Ham.

The Chinese idea that when eating fish, you should take a little from head and tail stresses overall balance. If you dine with Chinese friends, be careful never to leave your chopsticks sticking in cooked rice in a bowl. This is how people pray for and make sacrifices to ancestors.

So, every time you enjoy Chinese cuisine — without doubt one of the world best — just remember that Confucius once said, food is "people's Heaven."

Mommy, Where do Dumplings Come From?

I feel certain that in one of my mom's past lives she was Chinese and had her own restaurant. You couldn't tell it by looking at her of course, but her passion for cooking is proof enough for me. This is further endorsed by the magnitude of dumplings in our house. Whenever I come home the refrigerator is loaded with mom's homemade dumplings or Slavonic cousins, known as *vareniks*. When I visited Beijing for the first time in October 1999, I was astonished to hear that dumplings originated not in Siberia as most of Russians, Belarusians and Ukrainians believe but in China!

Jiaozi (the local name for dumplings) were popular in the Middle Kingdom as long as 1,700 years ago.

Dumpling is a favorite Chinese delicacy.

When I tell my Chinese and other foreign friends that I have always thought of dumplings as a Russian national dish, they raise their eyebrows and ask: "Really?" and rapidly go on to the next question: "Can you make them?" I have to answer honestly that I am good on theory, but my mom....

Sugar-coated hawthorn berries is one of the Beijing winter street favourites.

But my dear mom, maker of supreme dumplings, has no idea that some of Beijing's restaurants serve *jiaozi* with 130 different fillings, flavored with up to 200 spices. The most popular filling in Beijing's *jiaozi* is pork with cabbage or other vegetables: onions, carrots, coriander, chives and many more. Foreigners not accustomed to dumplings prefer the steamed buns known as *baozi,* a kind of hybrid so popular in the North made from steamed bread and a meat filling.

The Southern version of *jiaozi*, called *wonton* or *huntun*, is tiny dumplings with egg and meat fillings served in a rich broth. Some insist that the origins of the name of this dish are in the word *hundun* meaning cosmic chaos, and that adding dumplings to soup is like putting the universe in order. Cuisine using cosmic metaphors indicates just how seriously its host country takes food.

Dumplings in China symbolize unity, harmony and balance, which is why they are a must dish at Lunar New Year. This symbolism derives from the process of preparation, as all family members generally participate in "wrapping" *jiaozi*. This turns everyday meal into a joyful and festive event. Its shape is also significant. Dumplings at

Peking duck.

Lunar New Year are crescent-shaped, also similar to the form of a silver ingot, ancient Chinese money, inviting prosperity and wealth in the coming New Year. The name *jiaozi* is actually derived from that of the first paper money ever printed.

At the mention of "rice" people all over the world automatically think of China, but it is the staple food of South China, not the whole country. Northerners prefer, as mentioned, noodles, steamed buns. Their delicacies also include dumplings and spring rolls — tiny pancakes made of crispy dough with various fillings. But the main jewel in the crown of Northern cuisine is without doubt Peking duck.

This famous roasted duck was created by a Mr. Yang, purveyor of fatty birds, who upon deciding to change his occupation in 1864 opened the now

Not every chef will cut the famous Beijing duck as it is real art.

famous Quanjude Restaurant. He invited the best chefs from Shandong Province, famous for its refined dishes, sent out spies to steal the secrets of imperial cuisine and invented his own duck roasting technique. Initially the dish comprised the bird's crispy skin, served with shallots and special sauce wrapped in a small pancake. All the duck's other parts were used in dishes ranging from stew to soup. Duck's tongue and brains were (and still are) regarded as a delicacy.

During the 19th century foreign diplomats in Beijing tried this dish known as Peking duck, and it thereafter became hailed and sought after the world over. When George Bush senior, former president and father of the current president, worked in Beijing as leader of the US Liaison Office in China (at that time there were no diplomatic relations between the USA and China so neither country had the other's embassy) he developed a passion for the dish. Even today Bushes visit an American Chinese restaurant serving Peking duck at least once a month.

Hotpot is a great dish for keeping warm.

Anyone familiar with Chinese history is unsurprised by the strong Mongolian influence on Northern cuisine. The two most famous dishes — Mongolian barbeque and Mongolian hotpot — were originally soldier's fare cooked over campfires. Meat with vegetables were fried on shields (barbeque origins?), and in some cases boiled together in a helmet — the birth of hotpot.

Hotpot is a great dish for keeping warm during the cold winter days. It is cooked in a copper over an open fire. Diners throw paper-thin slices of mutton, vegetables, noodles and *tofu* into a boiling sauce, which hotpot aficionados swear is crucial to overall enjoyment of the dish. Thick and richly flavored, it is a mixture of sesame paste, garlic, Chinese chives, red fermented *tofu*, fish seasoning and Mongolian spices.

Old-time hotpot ingredients were various — from beef and rabbit ears, to fish heads, to black pudding. Today's hotpot is a sinicized version and demonstrates the essentially Chinese desire for balanced servings of meat and vegetables.

But you can never truly know Northern cuisine until you try the snacks sold on Beijing's streets. They are known as *dian xin*, a term that originates in the classical literary expression *diancai suixin*—"choose dishes according to the dictates of your heart." In ancient times the most famous confectionery came from Hangzhou and Chang'an (today's Xi'an) and the first person in Beijing to develop a passion for it was Empress Dowager Ci Xi. The court and commoners alike followed her lead.

Hotpot.

These snacks come in a great variety. There are, for example, *ai wo wo* — tiny balls made of glutinous rice dough with a red spot on top and various fillings; *wan dou huang* — small square cakes made of pea dough, a particular favorite of Ci Xi; *qie gao* — puff pie made of glutinous rice and red soy paste, to name but the three. If you are walking along the Beijing streets with a child you are unlikely to avoid buying a *tang hulu* — different fruits or big hawthorn berries on a stick and covered with caramelized sugar.

Deep-fried rolls with fillings of sweet bean paste.

My personal favorite street food is *jian bing*, a tasty and filling snack. It is cooked before your eyes so freshness is guaranteed. Liquid dough is poured on to a circular broiler, spread evenly with a spatula, and an egg or two (according to taste) beaten in. The mixture is then sprinkled with greens, smeared with various sauces and another crispy pancake of maize dough placed at its center. It is often folded in four and wrapped in thick brown paper. Armed with this mighty *jian bing* you are equal to all winter weather — even in Siberia!

What do Real Revolutionaries Eat?

Chinese cuisine in the western regions is proudly spicy. Its distinctive flavor comes from red-hot chili peppers, an ingredient first brought to China by Spanish merchants in the 17th century. But Sichuan cuisine was hot long before the Spaniards arrived. A collection of poems from the ancient state Chu entitled *Elegy to the South* reveals that natives of the area have been cooking with Sichuan pepper, cassia (local cinnamon), wormwood and other spices since 300 BC. Texts unearthed from Han Dynasty (260 BC-220 AD) tombs also describe rich, diverse and exquisite dishes flavored with exotic spices. Nowadays chili and garlic have supplanted some of the spices from former times, but Sichuan pepper, cassia, star-shaped anise, five spice powder and coriander still feature in local Sichuan cuisine.

The main purpose of northern Chinese cuisine is to retain body heat in cold weather. Sichuan dishes, on the other hand, are aimed at drying the body from the inside, bearing in mind the high humidity of this region. Hot chili in sultry and humid weather creates internal interstices that act as a cooling system. In winter chili warms the body from the inside, hastening blood circulation, promoting the metabolism and accelerating digestion. Also, as foodstuffs do not keep in warm climate, and the re-

Red pepper is the main ingredient of the cuisine in the western regions.

frigerator is a relatively recent invention, how did Chinese ancestors prevent food from going bad? With chili: a reliable destroyer of bacteria.

Sichuan Province is blessed with a subtropical climate and excellent irrigation, so fresh foodstuffs are plentiful all year round. Staples of the local cuisine are rice, vermicelli, pork, cabbage, white radish, fresh water fish and bean curd. Mountains densely covered in bamboo groves are the habitat for pandas, symbol of Sichuan and China. Bamboo is their staple food, and also a favorite item for human consumption, along with the various kinds of mushrooms, native-grasses and tree roots that enrich local dinner tables.

This mountainous region is also rich in all kinds of nuts, in particular walnuts, ginkgo and stone-pine. Long harsh winters oblige the Sichuanese to preserve vegetables, something they accomplish with salt, vinegar, oil and — of course! — indispensable chili.

Chairman Mao Zedong was born in Hunan and never lost his love of the local spice cuisine, insisting that: "Those who do not eat hot dishes are not real revolutionaries." It was only a few decades ago that genuine revolutionaries were temporarily based in Sichuan, so it is no surprise that the local cuisine's fame has spread all over China, along with Communist ideals and people's power. Chefs are very cautious when choosing ingredients and flavorings; every dish is cooked in its particular way. The Chinese western school of cooking is often referred to as the "cuisine of one thousand and one tastes." Among its most famous dishes are spicy pork, *gongbao jiding* — chicken fried with nuts and vegetables, chicken bites cooked with spices, and bean curd with chili and prickly ash.

Tofu cooked by a master is transformed into delicacies such as Pock-marked Wife *Tofu*, White Water *Tofu*, Pocket-Shaped *Tofu*, and Eight Treasure *Tofu*. Bean curd is by no means a Sichuan specialty; it is consumed all over China and is popular with vegetarians around the world. At times eating it can be an adventure.

Casserole of *Tofu* and Vegetables.

Tofu nao, for example, is a dish of bean curd in a rich brown sauce cooked with fine chopped meat, green cucumber and cloud- (or ear-) shaped wild fungus. It is one of Beijing's the most popular breakfast dishes and very nutritious.

People of Sichuan are very inventive when it comes to cooking and have created many unusual recipes. There is one local story of how somebody once threw a couple of small crucian carps into a jug of pickles, so adding a distinctive spiciness to an already hot dish. This unusual dressing, named "fish pepper," is added to onion, ginger, garlic, soy sauce, salt, sugar and vinegar, creating a whole range of dishes with "fish aroma."

Sichuan cuisine encompasses more than 20 methods of cooking, yet throughout all the spices used are basically the same; only the main ingredient changes. One method of cooking can, therefore, create a whole range of dishes. Take "fried rice with meat bites" as an example. First crunchy fried rice is placed on a plate, followed by a spicy condiment and only then are thin slices of meat added to make a delectable dish. When shrimps are substituted for meat another dish is created — "fried rice with shrimps." The dish thus changes according to the main ingredient.

When I think about Sichuan cuisine, the first thing that comes to mind is *yu xiang rou si* — straw-shaped slivers of pork with fish aroma. It was the first dish I ordered in Chinese and is my favorite of all, and after four years in China I like it just as much now as when I first tried it. I order it in every new restaurant I go to because each chef adds his own special something, so it tastes a little different each time. This is actually one of the reasons why I so like Chinese food and Sichuan cuisine in particular: for the surprises and discoveries that lurk in the most standard dishes.

Stir-fried Chicken with Chili Sauce and Peanuts.

Drink Tea and Fly like an Eagle

As home of the tea plant, China is synonymous with this refreshing beverage. A drink made from the leaves of the plant *Camellia Sinesis* is described in *Shennong Ben Cao Jing* (*Materia Medica of Shennong*) of 2737 BC as "health giving" and one that "brings joy to the heart." Tea drinking was strictly for medicinal purposes until the end of the Han Dynasty in 220. It then became an essential aspect of intellectual debate, particularly in the state of Shu of the Three Kingdoms Period (220-280) where it was preferred to wine. Buddhism has also played a supporting role in this Chinese love affair with tea. According to a legend, the very first tea seedlings sprouted from eyelashes of the monk Bodhidharma, an aid to staying awake during long nights of meditation. For centuries Chi-

Relishing tea.

nese simply boiled tealeaves in a pot like soup and did not use the infusion method until the 14th century. It was during the Song Dynasty (960-1279) that tea drinking became a stylized ritual and that a state monopoly on tea production and trading came into force.

Tea-drinking became fashionable in Europe and America only

in the 17th-18th centuries, when trading with China began. People think of tea as a traditional English drink, which is certainly true, but how did this come about? Tea was first drunk in China and next in India. It was expansion of trade and reduction in import tax in 1746 that gave birth to the famous British "tea at five o'clock" tradition.

There are five categories of Chinese tea. Most popular within China is green tea, which retains its original color, and whose leaves are heated to prevent fermentation or oil effusion in boiling water. The most famous green teas in China are Longjin (Dragon Well) from Zhejiang Province, Maofeng from Huangshan Mountains in Anhui Province and Biluochun from Jiangsu.

Black tea in China is called *hong cha* — "red tea." Its leaves are fermented before being heated and it contains oils that dissolve in hot water, giving it a darker color. This kind of tea making has only been popular in China since the 17th century. The finest of *hong cha* are Qihong from Anhui, Dianhong from Yunnan, Suhong from Jiangsu, Chuanhong from Sichuan and Huhong from Hunan Province.

Boccaro teapot.

The third category of tea is unique to China and has no equivalent in any other country. It is oolong tea, which is partially fermented and occupies an intermediate position between green and black tea. It appears after partial fermentation. Oolong specialists are all situated in China's southern provinces — Fujian, Guangdong and Taiwan. The most famous oolong tea is "Iron Guanyin."

Teahouse. Kashgar (Xinjiang Uygur Autonomous Region).

Compressed tea produced in briquettes is convenient for storage and shipping. Often referred to as "black," it is not the same as the black tea drunk in Europe. It is produced mainly in Hubei, Hunan, Sichuan and Yunnan provinces.

Aromatized tea is a mixture of tealeaves and flowers, although tea made exclusively from flowers is no rarity. Jasmine tea is most popular in northern China, where it is believed that aromatized tea improves the digestion through helping break down fats.

In many restaurants tea is served before anything else, regardless of whether or not it has been ordered, and is often free of charge. Diners order oily and spicy dishes without fear of gastric repercussions, as a drink of green tea ensures easy digestion.

To Chinese people, tea is like a faithful and beloved wife who commands complete loyalty. Virtually every citizen of the Celestial Kingdom has their favorite tea from which they seldom stray. They take it with them in a tea flask to work or public functions. It may be observed that televised participants in governmental conferences bring their own tea to place in the cups provided to be periodically topped up with boiling water. This is one attribute of tea particularly appreciated by thrifty Chinese: that a portion lasts for several hours and retains its quality.

There is a Chinese saying: "It is better to live three days without salt than one day without tea." Tea is considered a remedy for many diseases within traditional Chinese medicine. Practitioners insist that bitter tea relieves inflammation, prevents upset stomach, whets appetite, and restores good spirits. Tea is rich in vitamin C, which combats cholesterol, arteriosclerosis and hypertension. The vitamin P in tea helps clean blood-vessel walls and soften capillaries, and its other vitamins prevent formation of blood pigmentation and melanoma. Another tea ingredient, tannin, soaks up melanin and flushes it out of the body, keeping the skin soft and healthy looking. Tea also contains alkaline minerals that decompose fats and help

Everything is ready for tea ceremony.

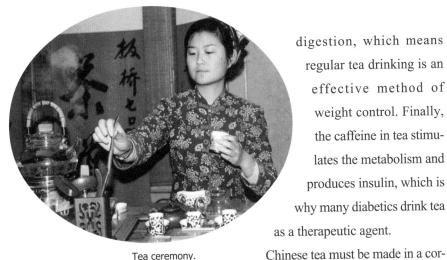

Tea ceremony.

digestion, which means regular tea drinking is an effective method of weight control. Finally, the caffeine in tea stimulates the metabolism and produces insulin, which is why many diabetics drink tea as a therapeutic agent.

Chinese tea must be made in a correct way, and great store has always been laid on implements and ingredients, the most important being, of course, water. By the 9th century tea-drinking connoisseurs had formulated 16 rules in regard to heating water, one of which was that it should be boiled over flames fueled by coal from the same area as where the tea plant originally grew. Well water being considered inappropriate, the best water was deemed to come from mountain springs containing melted snow and bamboo dew. Correct tea implements were also essential to a good cup. For a long time teapots were made of metal: gold, silver, copper, tin and alloys. During the Tang Dynasty (618-907), they were fashioned in white and grey-green porcelain, that, when tapped, emitted a sound like "sorrowful jade." Later black cups were used, and during the Ming Dynasty (1368-1644) white porcelain painted with cobalt became fashionable. It was at this time that ceramic teapots became commonplace.

Here's to happy tea-drinking!

Land of Wine and Poets

Scientists believe that the Celestial Kingdom has the longest history of strong beverages in the world. Wine producing started in China at the time of Shennong, more than 7,000 years ago. The term "wine" loses something in translation because the majority of Chinese wine is actually strong spirit that would be better described as vodka.

Yi Di and Du Kang are considered the originators of wine-making in China. According to ancient annals, Yi Di was ordered by Yu the Great to produce mellow wine from fermented glutinous rice. The

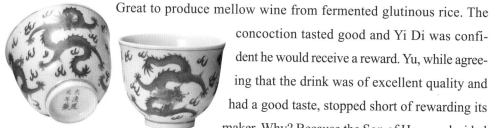
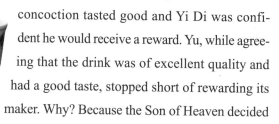

concoction tasted good and Yi Di was confident he would receive a reward. Yu, while agreeing that the drink was of excellent quality and had a good taste, stopped short of rewarding its maker. Why? Because the Son of Heaven decided that over indulgence in this new beverage could be dangerous — it could make a person (read — the monarch himself) loose his wits and inadvertently put the country at risk. Wise man!

Another wine creator, Du Kang, invented a formula for high quality liquor made of sorghum. As legend has it, one winter he put cultivated sorghum seeds in a hollow. The following spring he noticed a strong smell coming from it and was amazed to discover that the sorghum he left there had fermented. This accidental discovery inspired Du Kang to

Miao people traditionally greet their guests with a cup of good rice wine. Nanhua Village (Guizhou Province).

create an alcoholic beverage.

Many have heard about *sake*, a drink popular in Japan, but not so many know that this type of rice spirit exists in just one country other than Japan — China, the country of origin. Neither wine nor liquor, known as *jiu* in the Middle Kingdom, can approximately be translated as "strong beer." Ordinary beer or, to be more precise, its 4-5% strong prototype has been produced around the world over centuries. It was popular in Babylon and Egypt. Around 1500 BC it was used in China for sacrificial ceremonies. Production of *jiu* three times stronger than beer started in 1000 BC.

One amazing piece about alcohol production in China is that it was here that

brandy first appeared. Grapes, and drinks made from them, came to China with Arabian merchants in the second century BC. Chinese wine was first mentioned by Paracelsus. It caused a sensation in Europe, where technique of fermentation and distillation were as yet unknown. These days China produces brandy equal to that of France, only cheaper.

China began its classification of alcoholic drinks in the early Middle Ages. Most common is *bai jiu*, a white colorless spirit of 30 and higher degrees. On sale everywhere, it costs anything from a few yuan to thousands, depending on the brand. *Bai jiu* is an effective social tool; it can strengthen business alliances and turn yesterday's enemies into good friends. It is produced from cereals, usually sorghum and rice, and fermented with yeast and sugar. If first filtered and then bottled, a new kind of alcohol, *cui jiu*, is born. If distilled after fermentation you have *shao jiu* — a stronger, purer drink, generally found in the North. There have been dozens of popular and famous wines throughout Chinese history, many created by well-known scientists and poets. The Confucius family *jiu* — a strong, sweetish and fragrant drink produced in Qufu, home city of the great sage, for more than thousand years, is just one of them.

Du Kang is said to have invented liquor.

During the last couple of centuries classic wines (or vodkas, as we agreed earlier) have been made from sorghum. Most famous is that produced in Maotai, Guizhou Province, which is regarded as much a national treasure as is Longjing tea.

Wines from Maotai are the most expensive in China. They have been refined seven times and matured for no less than 3 years. Their potency varies from 39 to 55 degrees. Historians will proudly tell you how Maotai changed the world because the three cups drunk by

Tao Yuanming, a great Jin-dynasty poet, was a great lover of liquor. He once wrote a poem in praise of chrysanthemum.

Mao Zedong and Richard Nixon cemented Chinese-American relations and marked the start of a new era in world politics.

Maotai is, however, an expensive pleasure. It starts at 10 US dollars per bottle and for many years was used only at banquet for foreign dignitaries. Now it is available to all. But the real people's drink in China is *erguotou*, priced at a couple of yuan per half liter bottle. The most loved brand is "Hongxing" (Red Star) *erguotou*, and accounts for one-quarter of all alcohol produced in China. The word *erguotou* itself means "second distillation," which indicates its level of purity.

The Chinese have always considered wine mainly as a medicinal drink, and

Light beer is the favourite Chinese drink.

ancient medics used it to make many tinctures as remedies to promote vitality. Any Chinese medical reference book will list more than 70 kinds of medicinal wines. According to one ancient book, "Wine's ability to prevent diseases surpasses that of any diet."

Wine relaxes and opens the energy channels of the organism and promotes blood circulation. Distiller's yeast is frequently used as medicine to stimulate the appetite and improve digestion.

Fermented or distilled beverage can be used as a carrier for medicinal wine. Herbs and other ingredients are infused in wine, heated up or steamed. Every drugstore in China has bottles of wine containing pickled bees and snakes, scorpions and other creatures, along with herbs such as ginseng. The Chinese are convinced that the more poisonous the animal, the more healthier the wine made from it will make you. But be warned: in your rush to promote your health don't drink the whole bottle. The usual limit for imbibing "snake wine" is 100 g. More could be harmful to the health.

My advice for anybody planning to come to China is, don't bring your own tipple. This country has something for everything on that score.

Dinner Fit for an Emperor

All Chinese adhere to the old maxim: "Eating is paramount" and accordingly approach each meal in a serious and responsible manner.

Historians agree that the most famous and grand of all imperial banquets was that held in celebration of Emperor Qianlong's 80th birthday in 1791. Qianlong was the fourth Qing (1644-1911) emperor and had a broad range of attributes and talents. In 1795 on the day of the 60th year of his rule, Qianlong retired from state affairs to take up his lifelong passion — science.

River Eel in Sunflower Shape.

But in 1791 he was still very much ruler of the Kingdom of Heaven and the banquet in his honor was suitably sumptuous. The emperor's birthday was always a grand event of national celebration that lasted days. Even the supreme ruler himself took that day off from perusing lawsuits and official edicts. The Forbidden City would be decorated with lanterns and flags, so as numerous pavilions, altars and memorial arches constructed along the entire 15-kilometer length of road between the Forbidden City and the Old Summer Palace (Yuanmingyuan). Buddhist monks read sutras and prayed for the emperor's health, and concubines, relatives and officials were dressed in their most gorgeous raiment. Musical and operatic performances went on day and night.

On the day of his 80th birthday, Qianlong received relatives and high officials that had come to express their respect and tribute in the Hall of Supreme Harmony. Lunch was held in the Hall of Peace and Longevity, and in the evening there was a grand banquet in the Hall of Heavenly Purity. At its centre stood a huge table draped with a gem encrusted yellow tablecloth embroidered with dragons.

The banquet commenced as from the moment Qianlong took his seat. Altogether 129 courses were served, including 40 sorts of wine, 20 entrees, 4 soups, 4 appetizers, 4 kinds of fresh and 28 of dried fruits and 29 farinaceous dishes. The ware

Crispy Beef Rolls

from which the emperor ate and drank was made of bronze especially for the celebration and each tureen had a golden lid. The emperor ate with a spoon of rosewood and chopsticks made of gold inlaid ivory.

This celebration was named the Full Manchu-Han Banquet. It was distinct from run-of-the-mill banquets in having 129, rather than normal 108, courses comprising dishes from all over the Middle Kingdom.

During the Mongolian Yuan Dynasty (1279-1368) the increased influence of various ethnic groups was apparent

on banqueting tables of the country's nobility that groaned with Hui and Nüzhen dishes as well as Gaoli pies and Han specialties. Even then, attention was paid to healthy eating, the book *Principles of Healthy Diet* being very popular. The favourite Mongol dish was whole roasted lamb, and the famous banquet "Eight Treasures" course, comprising eight rare and expensive marine species, was also well-liked.

During the following Ming and Qing dynasties, the emperor's banquet reached its zenith. Dishes from all over the empire were served, many of them vegetarian. With the occidental voyages of Ming Dynasty Admiral Zheng He,

A party of court ladies, details from *Picture of Joy in the Palace*.

West European pastries began to appear on the table. Emperor Tianqi (1621-1627) of the Ming Dynasty liked to organize banquets on decorated boats floating on a lake. When Emperor Yongle (1403-1424) transferred the Ming capital from Nanjing to Beijing, the thousands of chefs that accompanied him adapted southern cuisine to northern taste and available foodstuffs.

It was during the Ming Dynasty that the famous "Eight Immortals' Table," a square table for eight, each place having special significance, appeared. The rule was to offer the south or west facing seat to the most honored guest, all other guests being seated according to rank and seniority.

Ming Dynasty emperors were noted gourmands, the Emperor's Entertainment Service employing 3,400 chefs to cook the most refined dishes.

In the first year of his rule, Emperor Shunzhi (1644-1661), founder of the Qing Dynasty, held the first Manchu banquet. They became the standard gastronomic celebration for such events as marriages, the first stage in the agricultural cycle, good hunting, and the vernal equinox. Manchu and Han officials would often invite one another for dinners and go to all kinds of culinary lengths in an effort to offer the most tempting delicacies.

Today, banquets are a luxury indeed, but a number of restaurants in Beijing nonetheless specialize in them. Other restaurants serve individual dishes of old palatial cuisine rather than laying out the full array in old impe-

rial style. A bowl of chicken soup in Yu Zhuan Tai Restaurant is made from poultry raised in Hebei Province and cooked for 10 hours. It exudes a mouthwatering aroma of chicken, ham and dried scallops.

These days, not many allow themselves the luxury of a full festive banquet. But it is always a pleasure to eat in any Chinese restaurant. With such a wide scope of delicious dishes, how can you go wrong?

Chinese people eat three times a day, and there are no fasting days on the Chinese lunar calendar. It is normal to start business discussions with a dinner but it is impolite to talk business while eating. So, if your partners invite you for dinner and you are in a

Han Xizai Gives a Night Party, showing life of nobles of the time, by Gu Hongzhong (937-975).

mood for a serious talk, be patient: there is a time and a place for everything.

The Chinese always choose dishes seriously and responsibly. Each person around the table is asked about dishes he/she prefers. Your hosts will be surprised to say the least if you do not show appropriate interest.

Food for Chinese is not simply a necessity but one of life's fundamental pleasures. Hence, they eat without haste and are willing to try as many dishes as possible. On festive occasions — as in old times — dishes can number in the hundreds. Today, and throughout history, meals start with the traditional "eight cold collations," among which are cold chicken, beans, black baked eggs, shrimps and various vegetables. Then there are the eight varieties of entrée, the last of which is often a whole fish. Rice is served in the middle of dinner and soup at the end of a meal to "precipitate" it, which I always find excellent for digestion. Usually dinner finishes with several kinds of sweets and fruits. But no coffee my dears, no coffee.

Red Lantern Streets — Chinese Style

When speaking of "red lantern streets," what's the first thing that comes to mind? Sordid alleys, haunted by ladies of the night? While "red lantern districts" both in the East and the West have something in common — namely pleasures, here in China, they are purely gastronomical in nature. Nearly every Chinese restaurant hangs large red lanterns at the doorway, and the more of them you see, the bigger the treat you are in for.

In many Western countries, Chinese restaurants do not enjoy the best reputation — they are regarded as noisy and poorly decorated, with their oil-cloths, plastic chopsticks, and cheap

Dongzhimennei Street in Beijing is famous for its numerous restaurants.

pictures. But to my mind, it is, once again, simply a difference in attitude, or, if you like, a difference of culture. In the West, people visit restaurants not just to eat, but also to socialize. In my home country, as well as in neighboring Russia and Ukraine, people can be seen dancing in restaurants. And around Beijing's Yabaolu district, there are indeed Russians dancing in restaurants there—come and see for yourself! But for the Chinese, the first and foremost reason they come to restaurants is... good food. Everything else, including décor, is secondary. Here, restaurants' opening hours are set according to Chinese people's eating habits. It can be difficult to find an open restaurant to "socialize" or dance in after 22:00. There are some exceptions of course, namely hotels, Yabaolu

"Russian" district and the famous Ghost Street in Dongzhimennei. In the daytime, between 14:00 and 17:00, restaurants are usually closed — Chinese people don't dine during these hours. Good restaurants in this country are not necessarily the most aesthetically pleasing ones, but they are easy to find. A dead giveaway would be a string of people lined up outside, and a packed parking lot.

These days, there are many excellent restaurants in Beijing

Restaurants on Dongzhimennei Street are very popular with locals as well as tourists.

that cater to every taste and wallet! You can find a simple dinner on the side of the road, where you can eat a huge plate of the best dumplings on earth for just 2 yuan, or you can go to a fancy restaurant and dine on Shanghai cuisine, but be prepared to shell out over 800 yuan for that luxury.

Beijingers are truly spoilt for choice. Statistics show that more and more people are eating out, and cooking less at home. This is true not only for weekends and holidays — every day, restaurants are packed.

Competition between local eateries is fierce. Nearly every street has 10 to 15 restaurants in a row, and each one does its best to lure customers. Don't be surprised if you feel someone tugging at your arm in a bid to entice you inside — it's their job!

In the evening in many cities, streets turn into restaurants with a big variety of foods.

Chinese customers have a curious characteristic unknown in Western countries — they order too much food. First of all, it is because the Chinese attach a lot of value to the concept of keeping "face." When inviting guests and friends out to dinner, the Chinese do not view it simply as "eating together." People come to restaurants (in many cases, expensive ones) to strengthen friendly ties and to do business. A big banquet is therefore considered a good investment. Impressive banquets in China are similar to lengthy business negotiations in the West, so Chinese hosts tend to splash out on

these occasions. Western partners should not regard their Chinese hosts as greedy — that would ruin both the friendship and the business deal. The reason behind the phenomenon is simple. The hosts feel that if all the food is gone at the end of the meal, their guests might think they are stingy. And in many cases, the company foots the bill. Every year, Chinese companies shell out an estimated US $12 billion on these banquets, but they are not overly concerned — it is viewed as a necessary investment.

Putting aside restaurants, white tablecloths, the obliging and sometimes even pushy waiters, it is easy to have a bite on the streets in Beijing. At the center of the well-known Wangfujing Street, there is the famous food alley. Nearby is an evening food market, known as the "Glutton's Stall" among the city's Russian community. Here you can buy and try all the favorite local dishes. After visiting these two markets, you will have a great impression of the diversity of Chinese gastronomy. Curious foreigner can pick up a *yang za sui* — goat's intestines, *zha go go* — skewered cicadas,

cockroaches or silkworms. These markets would definitely satisfy even the most adventurous gourmet.

And don't forget about teahouses. As you have already read in this book, tea drinking in China is a ritual, a demonstration of class and refined taste. Chatting over a pot of tea is very popular pastime among Chinese, and in the past, they would start the day with a visit to a well-known teahouse. Teahouses are the Chinese

answer to French cafés and English pubs. People come here not just for tea, but also to discuss local news or to have furious political debates.

These days, teahouses offer more than just a tasty beverage. Many now put on acrobatic shows, or have musicians, and you can have a very good time with your friends. Heads of state frequent Beijing Lao She Teahouse — their kind hosts take them there to enjoy local traditions and culture. I have also been there, and I'd recommend the place, for the excellent tea, the atmosphere and the variety show program.

There are literally thousands of restaurants and teahouses in Beijing — again you are spoiled for choice. If you can't be in China for too long, don't waste your time looking for Western restaurants. First they are much more expensive than the Chinese ones, and second you can eat your usual fare back home. Another reason is that the taste of many well-known dishes is different. Nearly all Western restaurants cater for local tastes and this results in sweeter and less pigment flavor. Even McDonald's burgers are a bit different!

Speaking of McDonalds, if you ask a Chinese to point you to a Western restaurant, I'm sure that 90 percent will

point towards McDonald's. It is here that whole families come to relax and have a good time, while young people come to date, celebrate birthdays and other holidays. Even business meetings are held here.

If you are interested in Chinese cuisine, may I take the liberty of offering one opinion? The only place in the world to eat truly authentic Chinese food is... China. There are certainly plenty of Chinese restaurants around the world. I have dined Chinese-style in London, New York, Minsk and Moscow. Now however, I am certain that the best place to get the real thing is China itself. I don't know the reason behind it — maybe it's the special air or the less than sterile that add a special flavor to the dishes, but you have to come here to taste the difference. So, welcome to Beijing!

Eating for Health

To the Chinese people, the function of food goes far beyond that merely filling the stomach. It is also essential for maintaining a healthy organic balance, reinforcing immunity and — last but not least — avoiding unnecessary visits to the pharmacy. Putting their money where the mouth is, Chinese people drink green tea to improve their digestion and eat special porridge to keep warm during cold winter days. There is a special term in Chinese — *yaoshan* or medicinal food — for dishes with medicinal functions.

In ancient times, the Chinese believed that treatment of any disease consisted of three stages. The first was *yaoshan* — medicinal food, the second *daoying* — physical exercise. The third, drugs, was considered a last resort if the first two failed. As traditional Chinese medicine (TCM) still follows these rules, it may be assumed they are effective. Any TCM practitioner will tell you that medicine and food share the same origins, which is why an everyday meal can also be of medicinal value.

According to ancient theory, the body is an organic whole. If any part of it doesn't work properly within the overall regime, the body becomes unbalanced and the person falls sick. Medical remedies opposite in nature to the illness should be prescribed in order to return the body to a balanced state. For example, medication considered hot by nature is used to treat diseases cold by nature.

Dishes are varied in nature as medicaments, but as food attributes are weaker than those of drugs, a proper diet can cure minor illness over a long period of

time. In treatment of serious illnesses, a proper diet acts as a supplement to medicine. In any event, Chinese doctors insist that a proper diet is in itself an excellent preventive remedy.

The recommended dietary regime comprises five tastes: sour, bitter, sweet, pungent and salty, and four natures: cold, hot, warm and cool. The five tastes determine how a food or drug affects the organism. For example, pungent food promotes circulation and evaporation of vital energy *qi*. Bitter tasting food opens blocked centers and promotes healthy bowels movement. Eating sour dishes accumulates and concentrates vital energy, and salty food alleviates all feelings of heaviness. The four natures are effective in treating diseases through being opposite in na-

Broth of Chinese Wolfberries and Pork Shreds.

ture to them, and each of the four seasons has associations with a particular organ.

Summer corresponds to the heart, autumn to the lungs and spring to the liver. As the heart is hot by nature, it is considered advisable to eat cold, bitter food in summer. Considering the time to accumulate vital energy, dishes eaten in autumn should be more nutritiously sour and sweet. Illnesses most likely to strike in this season are respiratory infections, but eating properly and drinking plenty of water fends them off. Spring is the best season to replenish the liver and winter is the time to nourish your kidneys.

Broth of Asparagus and Duck Meat.

All food possesses healing properties. Take, for example, the radish. According to Chinese tradition, this product is sweet and pungent by nature and with no harmful elements. Raw radish promotes saliva secretion and alleviates dryness in the body. It improves digestion, reduces heat (*shanghuo*), assists circulation of vital *qi* energy and dissolves phlegm.

One of the most popular street snacks sold all over the country from autumn to spring is hawthorn coated in caramel on a stick. Nowadays, it is made from other fruits: oranges, strawberries or kiwi, but traditional *bingtang hulu* is the hawthorn version. The best time to try it is Chinese New Year, a time of widespread gastronomic indulgence, because this fruit kebab improves digestion. The health-giving properties of hawthorns were, incidentally, defined centuries ago by famous Doctor Li Shizhen (1518-1593).

My mom taught me many useful things. One is that people should always keep a set of fundamentals in the kitchen. That they include salt, sugar, cereals and flour is no surprise but to my great surprise thus "must have" list includes walnuts, not commonly found in my home country Belarus. But, as ever, mom was right. And it was in China that I understood why.

According to TCM theory, walnuts are by nature sweet and slightly warm and are good for the lungs and kidneys. They also provide essential energy for metabolism and blood circulation and strengthen the reproductive function. Eating walnuts on a regular basis improves the skin, stops the hair going gray, warms the lungs and inhibits coughs. One particular anecdote describes the walnut's healthy effects:

An aged imperial court official had a cough for so long that he became too weak even to take medicine. Imperial medics prescribed him a mixture of three walnuts, three pieces of raw ginger and a cup of warm water to drink every evening before going to bed. He soon recovered.

Another example of dietary healing powers is the chestnut. Fried and sugared chestnuts are a favorite Parisian delicacy and are widely enjoyed in North China. From late autumn to early spring Beijingers can be seen eating chestnuts with relish. As we now know, the Chinese always have a reason other than liking a flavor for eating particular foods. As long ago as the Tang Dynasty (618-907), Doctor Song Simiao confirmed that chestnuts are good for the kidneys.

Chestnuts are salty and warm, just what TCM doctor orders for the kidneys in winter. They are especially beneficial to arthritis sufferers because healthy kidneys add strength to bones and tendons.

In traditional terms, winter is the time to accumulate energy so as to

Taro and Duck Soup

be strong and robust in spring. Black sesame and other black products can also be beneficial as they nourish the five internal organs
(heart, liver, spleen, lungs and kidneys), strengthen muscles and
the spirit too. It is also widely believed that black foods are beneficial for weak, sick and aged as well as to those whose hair is
turning gray or falling out.

It is plain to see that the Chinese lay great store on a good
digestion. They strongly believe that a properly functioning stomach inhibits disease of all kinds and that it is the straight track to a
fresh complexion and good health. I am always envious of the firm
healthy skin that all Chinese women seem to have. They assure me
that their beauty care is largely a proper diet — plenty of vegetables
and green tea. You can verify this for yourself but I assure you that
Chinese food theory works — I have already checked it.

图书在版编目（CIP）数据

生活中的中国文化与智慧／（白俄）朴列思卡切付斯卡娅 著.
－北京：外文出版社，2005
ISBN 978－7－119－04242－8
I. 生... Ⅱ.朴...Ⅲ.传统文化－简介－中国－英文
Ⅳ.G12

中国版本图书馆 CIP 数据核字（2005）第 111092 号

英文审定	王明杰
特约审读	李　霞
摄　　影	Inesa Pleskacheuskaya（白俄）　　Mikhail Penyevskoi（白俄）
	邓　佳 鲁忠民 孙树明 刘春根 国务院新闻办图片库 等
责任编辑	蔡莉莉
封面设计	华审视觉
装帧设计	北京京鲁创业科贸有限公司
印刷监制	张国祥

生活中的中国文化与智慧

（白俄）伊娜莎·朴列思卡切付斯卡娅　著

*

©外文出版社
外文出版社出版
（中国北京百万庄大街 24 号）
邮政编码　100037
外文出版社网址 http://www.flp.com.cn
外文出版社电子信箱 info@flp.com.cn
　　　　　　　　　sales@flp.com.cn
北京外文印刷厂
中国国际图书贸易总公司发行
（中国北京车公庄西路 35 号）
北京邮政信箱 399 号　邮政编码　100044
2007(小 16 开)第 1 版
2007 第 1 版第 1 次印刷
（英）
ISBN 978－7－119－04242－8
09800
7－E－3697P